I0833502

On An April Mourning

First Edition, 2023

www.zoerichesart.com

ISBN: 979-8-218-31677-8

Cover Design and Artwork by Zoë Riches
Written, Designed, and Curated in its Entirety by Zoë Riches

Poetry is authentic in nature. It is up to you how you interpret it.

ON AN APRIL MOURNING

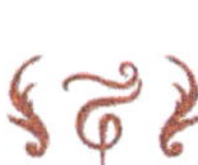

For ***you***

and for those with hearts swollen and overflowing
for someone that is just beyond their reach.

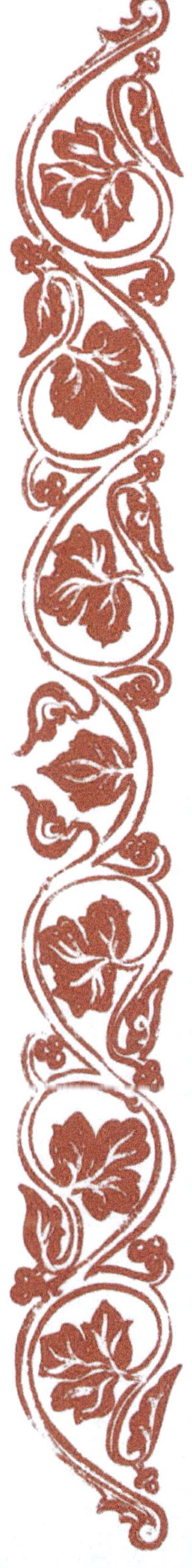

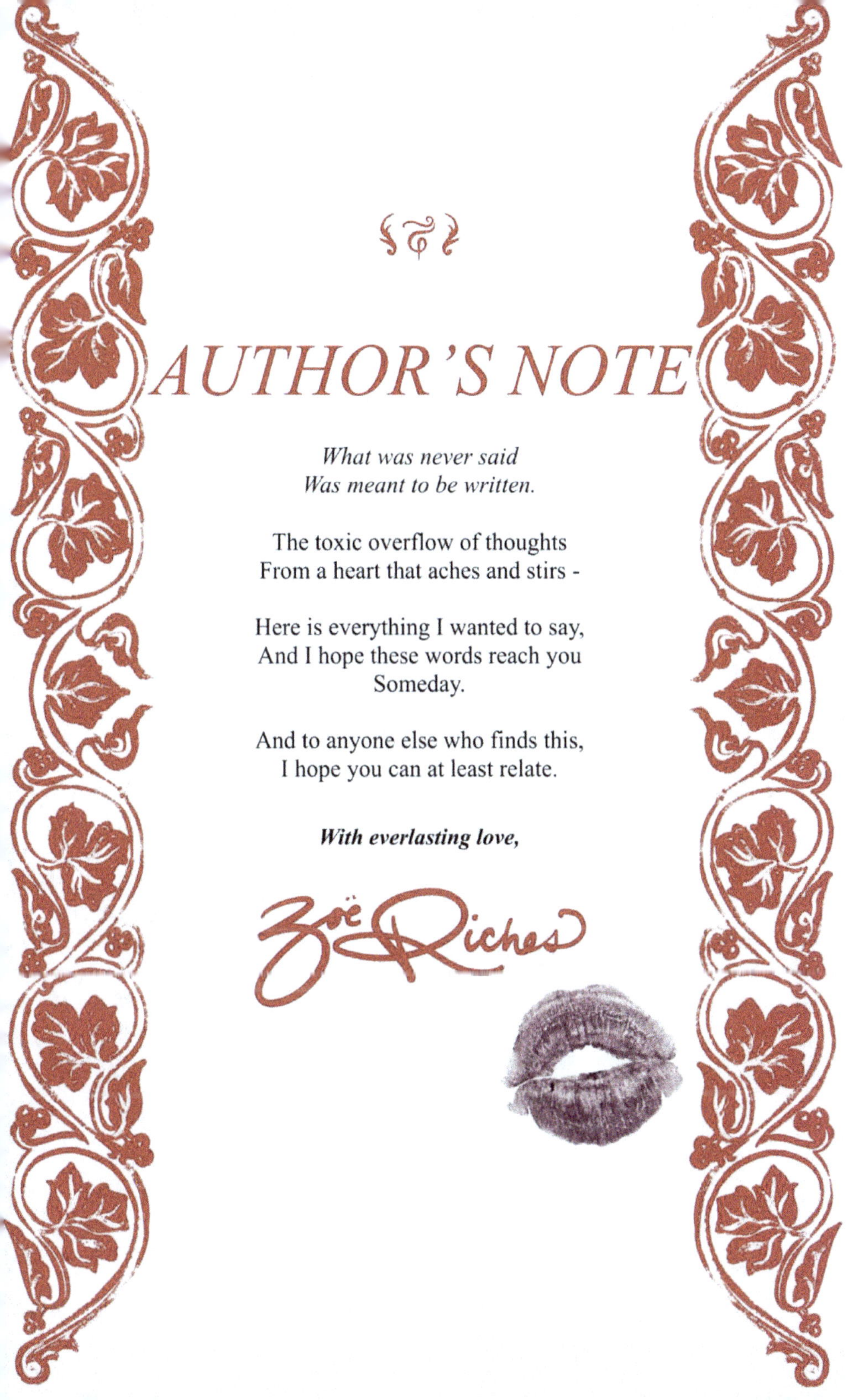

AUTHOR'S NOTE

What was never said
Was meant to be written.

The toxic overflow of thoughts
From a heart that aches and stirs -

Here is everything I wanted to say,
And I hope these words reach you
Someday.

And to anyone else who finds this,
I hope you can at least relate.

With everlasting love,

CONTENTS

iii - Stargirl

THE STARS OF DAWN
SOMEDAY WINTER WILL BE OURS
MAN FROM MARS
THE WILLOW TREE
ST. JAMES INFIRMARY BLUES
AEROPLANE OVER THE COUNTRYSIDE
GAS STATION ROSES
27
THE LOVE WITCH
GODHOOD IS MY HEART
EVANESCENT AS SMOKE FROM PARTED LIPS
CRUMBS
RAISON D'ÊTRE
STAR GIRL MANIFESTO
OUTSTRETCHED INTO THE ETHER

INTERLUDE

iv - Turn Me Into a Flower

AFTER WE PARTED WAYS
LUNAR DESTRUCTION
DON'T FORGET ME NOW THAT WE'RE APART
YOU.
THE CURSE OF A FREE WOMAN
INSIDE V. OUTSIDE
MAYBE I'M NOT REAL
SOME WORDS FROM THE ENVELOPE
70 CANDLES
MY FIRST WITHOUT YOU DREAM
THE HILLS
WINTER SOLSTICE
ASHES OF LOVE LETTERS
PRETTY LIKE THE GIRLS IN CALIFORNIA
I WAS ONCE A SPRING CHILD
IF IT RAINS AGAIN

EPILOGUE - I AM NEWNESS

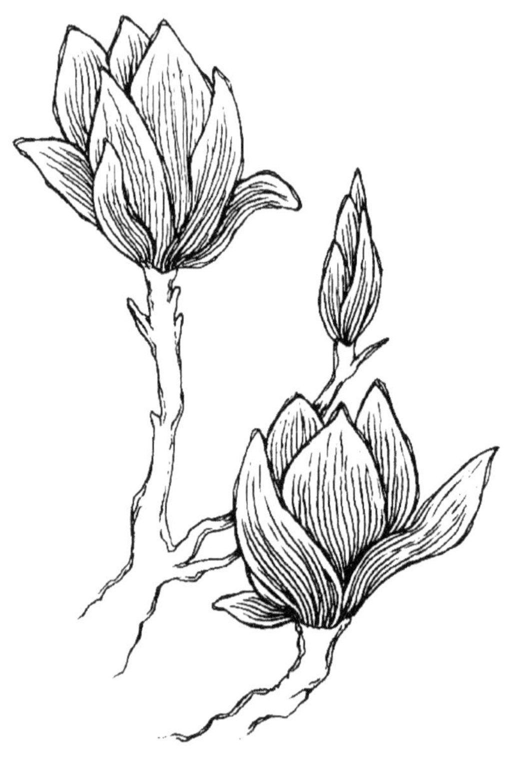

PREFACE

He said,
"This is extremely dramatic."
And I wasn't quite sure what he meant—
I was just in a moment of
Pure self-alignment.

I had found myself in the bathtub
Up to my shoulder blades in
Soothingly warm water
Wearing a black long-sleeve
Crop top and red
Lace underwear
Sipping from an opaque
Champagne glass
Half-full of grocery-store-bought
Top-shelf Riesling,
Tipsy and fighting off a
Panic attack,
My heart thunderously
Bumping in my
Back & neck & ears
When I had called him in
To write down the words
And phrases I didn't
Want to forget.

And he drunkenly scribbled them down
On a junk-mail envelope he dug out
Of the top drawer of his desk
With a red glitter gel pen he found
On mine.
"That's why I loved you,"
He continued.

I rolled my eyes.
We had just spent the last week
In each other's heartbreak.
"Oh shut up!"
I whined.
"I'm writing a book."
How *libra* of me.

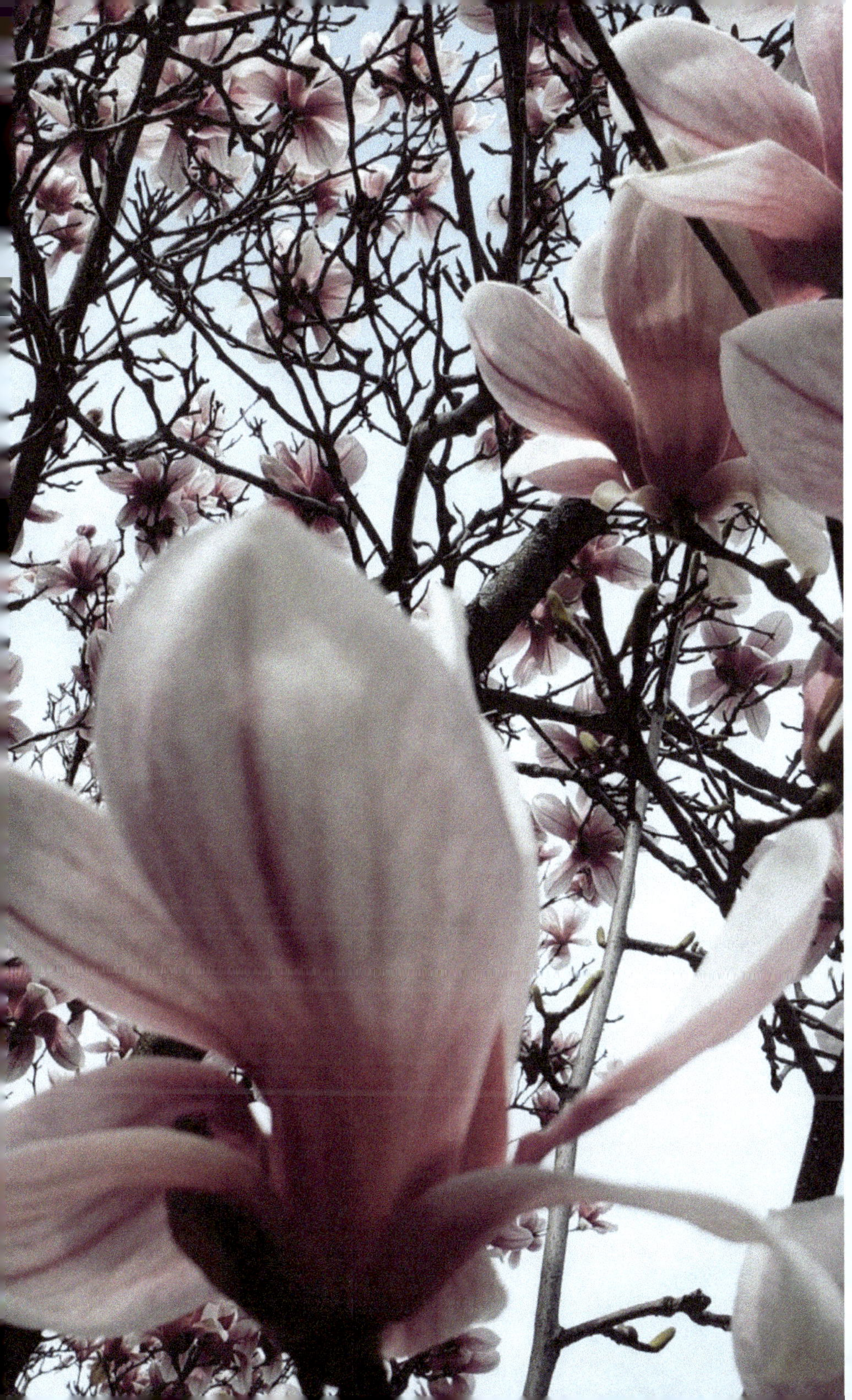

CENSORED FOR YOUR READING PLEASURE

These poems are (mildly) censored
because I am still somehow frightened
of my own truth—
though I still hope and pray that
this letter,
this bible,
this loving act of devotion
finds its way into your hands—

Your hands,
the hands that I dream about,
the hands that make me squirm
with devilish thought—

As you tenderly thumb through her pages,
caress her covers,
run your fingers down her spine;
please think of me and
my eager skin
(if this does find *you.*)

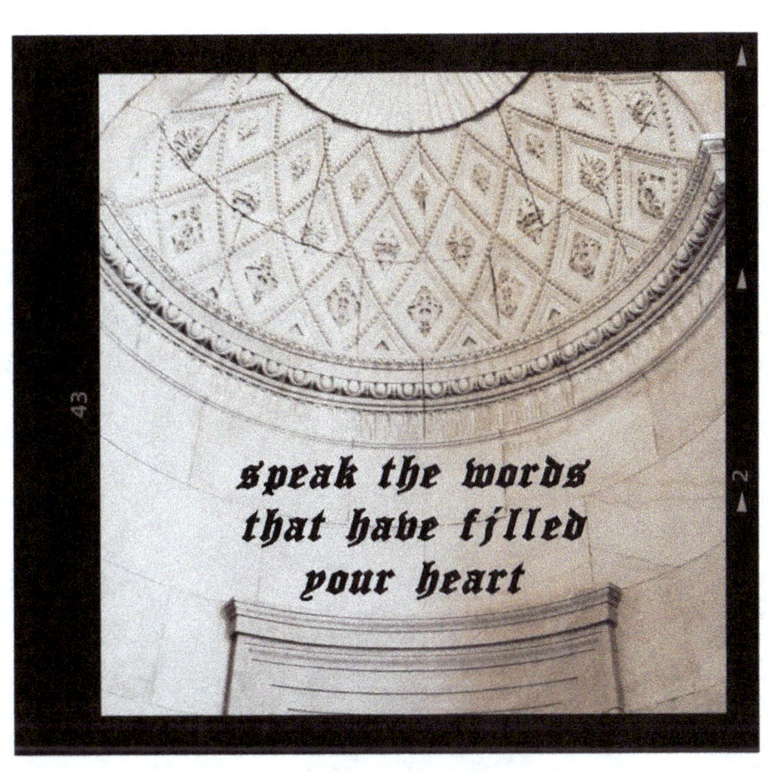
43
2
speak the words
that have filled
your heart

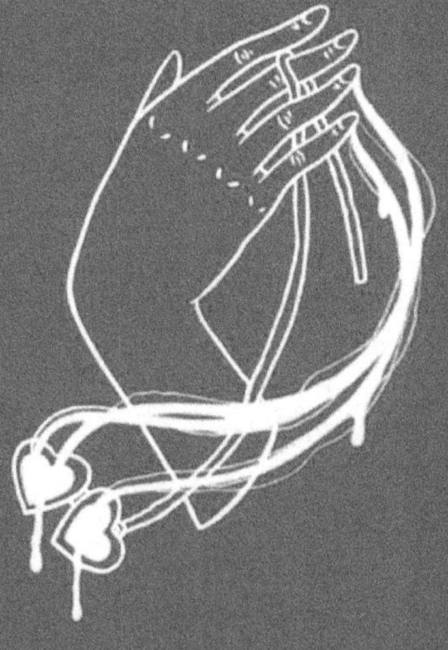

TO THE END OF THE EARTH

- i -

ON THAT APRIL MORNING

It rained heavily the night I finally saw you.
And you kissed me gently then passionately through the ether.
You held me firmly and
loved me intensely.

It poured the night I saw you,
pouring and pouring through the gutters and
rushing and rushing down the streets.
With a head still buzzing from pain
and lips reddened from the cold,
I saw you and
felt you solidly in my dreams.

I tossed in the sheets ~~I shared with another man~~.
I winced from the pleasure of the images.
All the while, it rained and poured on the streets below.

[My heart,
Booming and pulsing in my ears ;;
My lungs,
Gasping for the air from yours.]

It rained heavily the night I really saw you.
The way you hold yourself,
The angles of your hands,
The color of your beautiful eyes,
And your shining smile—
It all haunted me.

I will always wonder if you had really seen me too.

I will always wonder if I touched you through the ether too.

I will always wonder if you thought of me
Tangled in the sheets ~~you shared with another woman~~.

Because when the Sun finally rose,
It was raining magnolia petals—
Dusty pink and white down the quiet streets.
And with every falling petal I whispered to myself ::
"He loves me, he loves me not."

We were still kids,
Unsure of our place in the universe,
Watching the stars colliding with the clouds that draped
Over our dusty pink city.

It rained magnolia petals when I finally saw you,
With a heart full—
Devilishly infernal but somehow godlike,
A taste of blood wine
Like a dripping fountain
Racing with nerves,
For you became my deepest desire,
My ultimate *Secret*—
Tucked away in the locket that hung from my neck;;
My neck – that I wished to be covered in your kisses.

It poured magnolia petals,
Dusty pink and white,
With a glass-brimming heart,
On that April morning.

THE MOON, MY MOTHER

The Moon faintly whistled in my ear,
beckoning me.
With a light touch and gentle whisper
she said,
"I see your heart aches,
swelling beyond its capacity,
filling your chest
and stretching your frame."

My eyes glistened in her sweet light.
"You are brimming with constellations
that desire freedom from your eyes."

The truth hides
from the easiest solution.
And with her I wonder
if she watches my dreams
among the cloudless night sky
as the stars gather
with their curious minds,
eyes wide with anticipation.

She said,
"A mother knows,
A sense of struggle
And a lack of happiness,
It is evident in
your spiraling patterns."

I don't dance like I used to,
And I long for a freedom I once had,
A new land with many sacrifices,
A hauntingly sick mind.
It's true.

“The whirlwind in your stomach,
Your palpitating heart,
The way you sing to yourself
When you’re alone with your thoughts,
Is a longing you must accept.”

My heart stopped with the thought,
Death, The Tower, The Lovers.
With destruction,
May there finally be peace.

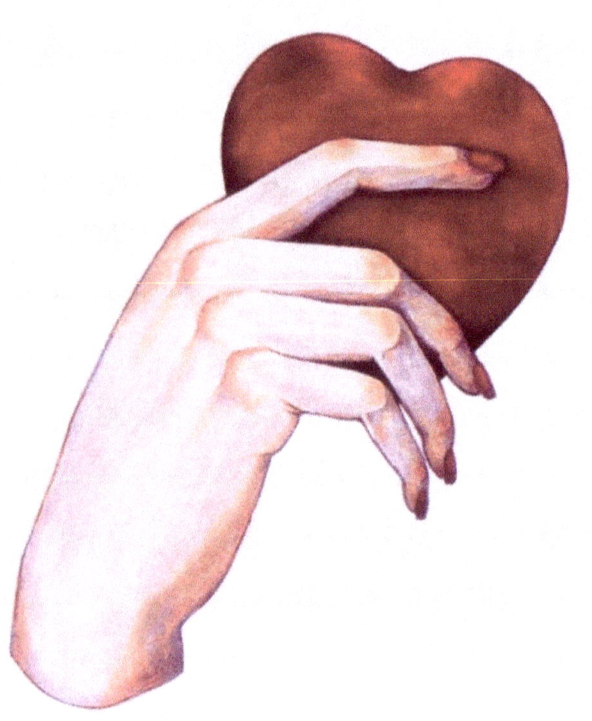

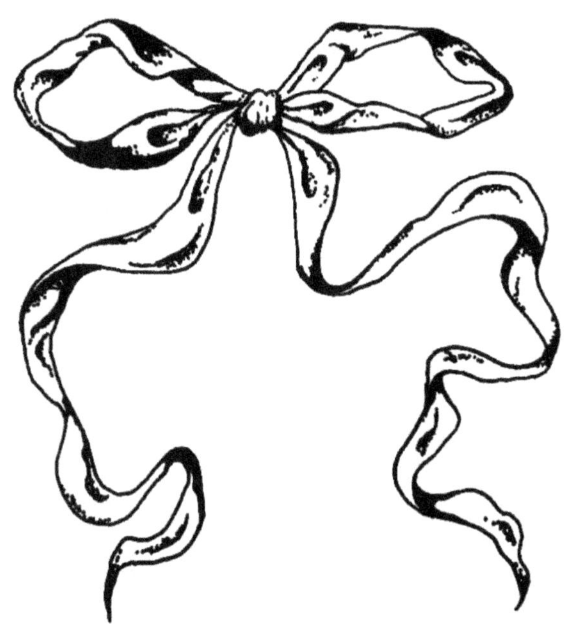

I WISH I HAD BEEN *THE* MAGNOLIA TREE

I wish I had been the magnolia tree to watch a young woman fall helplessly in love.

I wouldn't have spent my nights praying for more dreams of you,
nor would I have ached and cried as intensely.

Instead, I would have simply spent my days basking in the Sun,
Drinking up the rainwater brought in from the Bay,
Waxing and Waning with the Moon.

I wish I had been the magnolia tree,
Sprouting and shedding hypnotic wonder every spring,
Standing tall and full every summer,
Drifting off into slumber every autumn.

THE CHARLES RIVER ESPLANADE

The Charles River
is not daunting at first,
unless you fear the water.
I always dreamt of swimming down it
rather than across.
I imagined its current was strong enough
to take me to you—
but watching it flow,
it reminded me of molasses & sludge.

It felt as though
The Charles River
separated us—
though I think I always knew
in the back of my mind
that it didn't.
I was afraid you were downstream
on the other side ;;
I didn't know you were standing next to me
the entire time.

Whenever I gazed at
The Charles River
and watched how slowly it seemed to move,
I would cry my tears into the current
& pray that somehow they would reach you.

And although
The Charles River
did not actually divide us,
I unknowingly allowed it to.
And when I watched the setting sun at
The Riverside;
oh, how the colors amazed me—
a hypnotic dance between the
bursting rays of pink
and the lustful temptations of the night—
it reminded me of the dance we did,
passing up & down along the side of
The Charles River Esplanade
and missing each other every time.

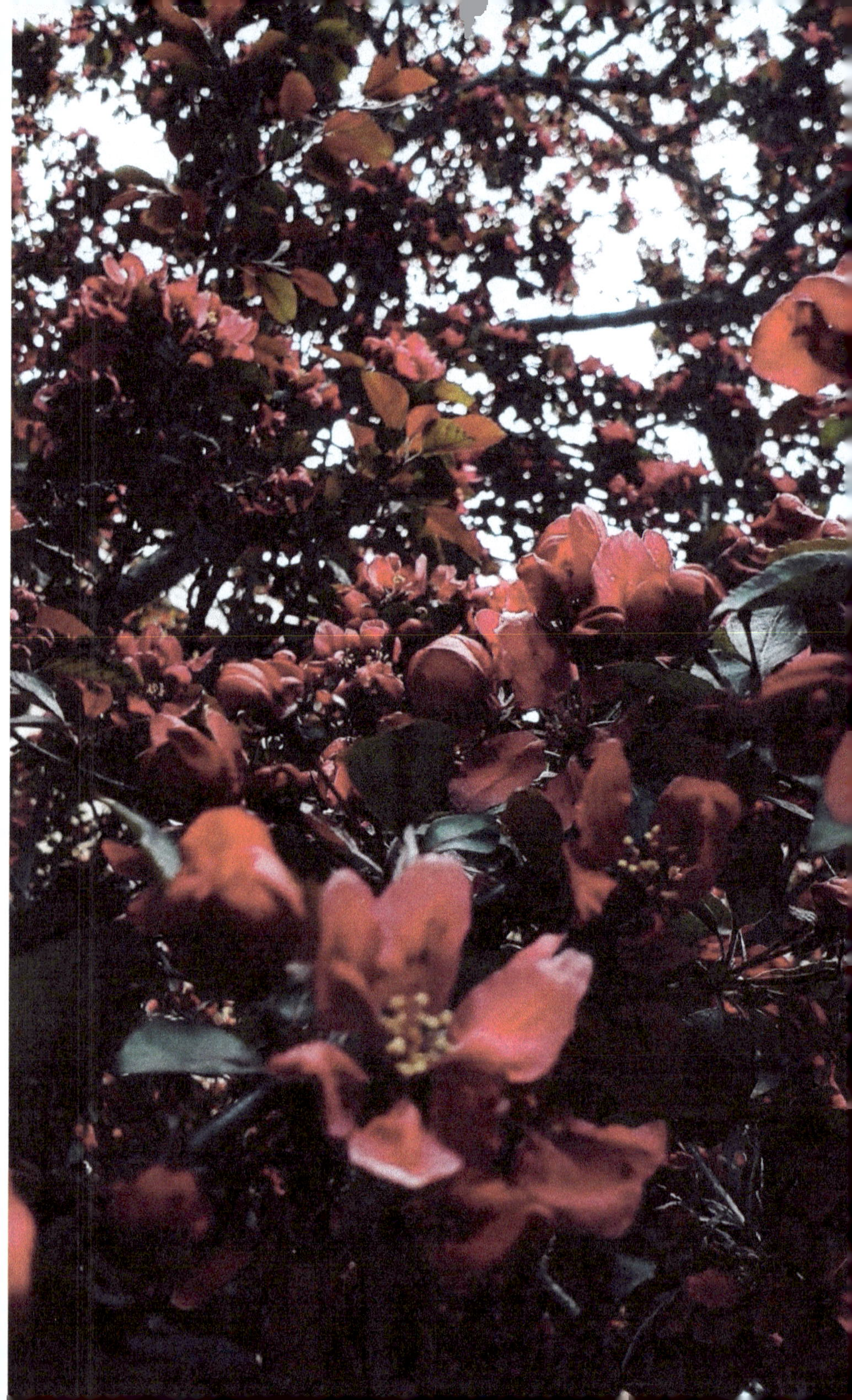

AN ODE TO HEARTBREAK

I have noticed lately // that we don't yearn & long anymore. // We don't rip our hearts out // and bleed profusely onto the cold streets. // We don't cry & wail & scream // to the full Mother Moon // like we probably should. // We don't beg & plead // with the Gods // to grant us our true loves. // I feel crazy at times, // Destroyed and Defeated // with how much I yearn for you, // believing no one else // feels the way I do. // Not even you. // But I would rather shred my skin // with my breaking fingernails // than feel nothing for you, // than to be bored & boring. // Because the Great Human Experience // is feeling painful life // rather than of dull death.

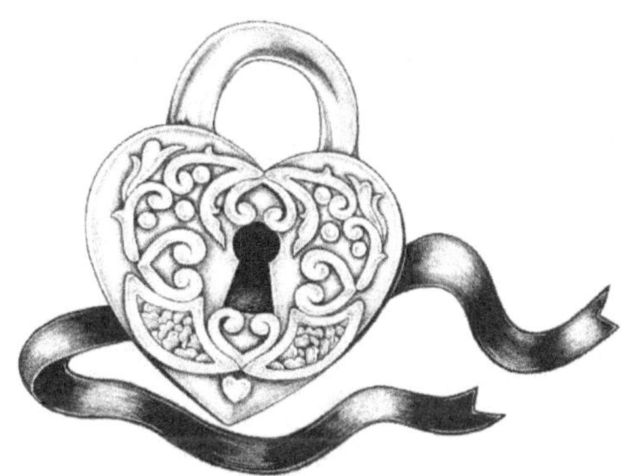

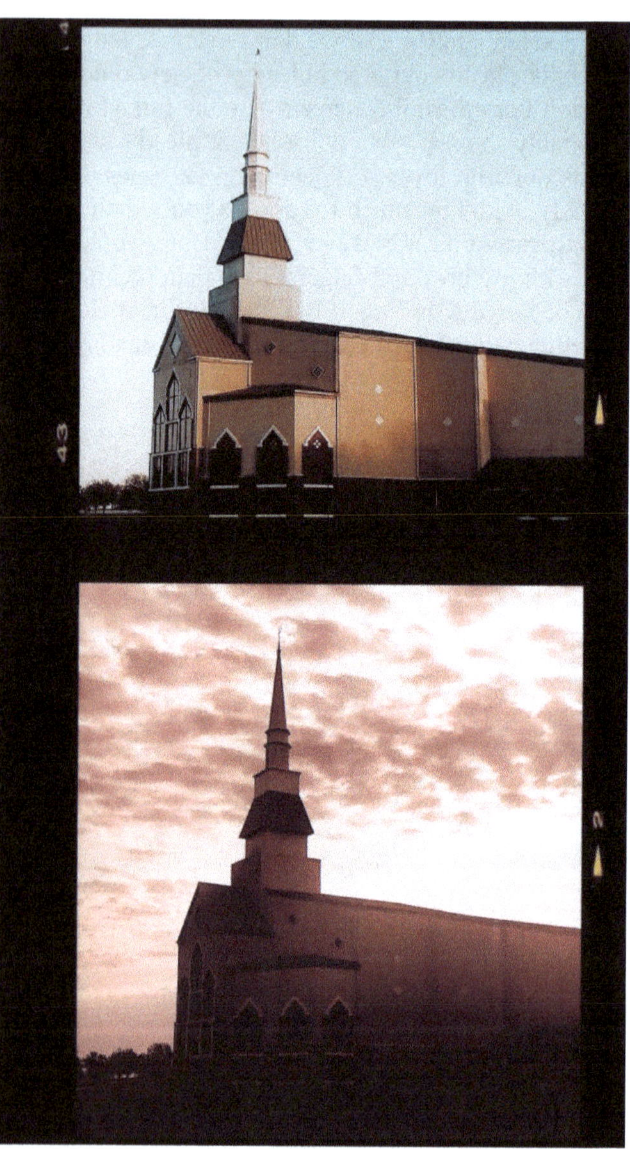

THERE IS GREAT STRENGTH IN SOFTNESS

I found you in a dream I wish never ended—
and when we first met,
years ago, now,
you were still a child ;;
a timid boy with talented hands and
a shaky voice.

I've always resented the Hollywood Hills for
taking you away from me—
hollyhock and lilac and wisteria,
and all the little flowers in between
dancing in the summer breeze.

The magnolias were my favorite,
they always reminded me of you,
and how the beautiful blossoms would
rain down onto the streets resembled
all the nights I yearned for you.

There is great strength in softness,
I'm just learning that now,
and how I long for your warm tenderness
inside my quivering arms.

Love and lust come as a pair,
but my heart had turned them into one.

Is this great strength or am I
riddled with sickness?

This almost feels like a plague I will never quite heal from.

MY ENDLESS SEA

I have always wondered about you,
My endless sea,
My endless mystery.

I've always wanted to know
What it would be like to
Kiss you underwater—

To feel your soft skin and
Glide my fingers through
Your luscious hair

Without being able to breathe—
To press myself against your
Solid form in minimal gravity.

To dance with you,
My endless mystery,
In the endless sea.

And if only you could see into my eyes,
Really see their true color
As I gaze deeply into yours—

Maybe the words will spill through them
Instead of our drowning lips
That I hope will always be connected.

Breathe my air into your lungs and
Taste its sweetness,
And I will catch your breath in my frame—

A constant flow, back and forth,
Until there is nothing left
But the water that surrounds us—

Pushes us together.
My ribs will open like a birdcage,
And we can wrap each other up in the

Fragile little bones.
I'd love to see the bubbles dancing
All around us

As we close into each other.
How I wish to be within you,
Around you,

My endless sea,
My endless mystery.

How I want to swim in your vastness,
Drink up your kisses,
And drown in your embrace.

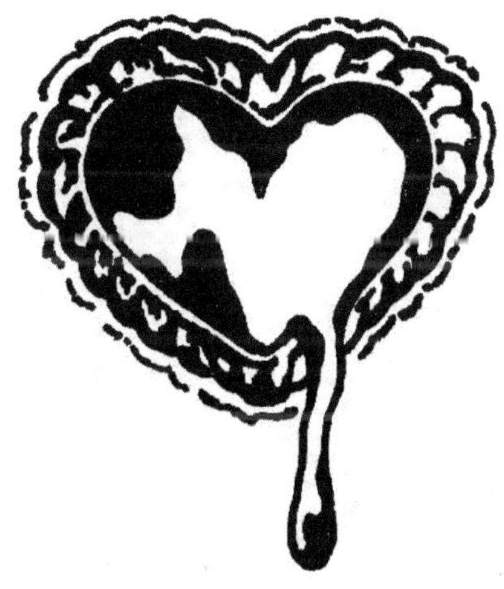

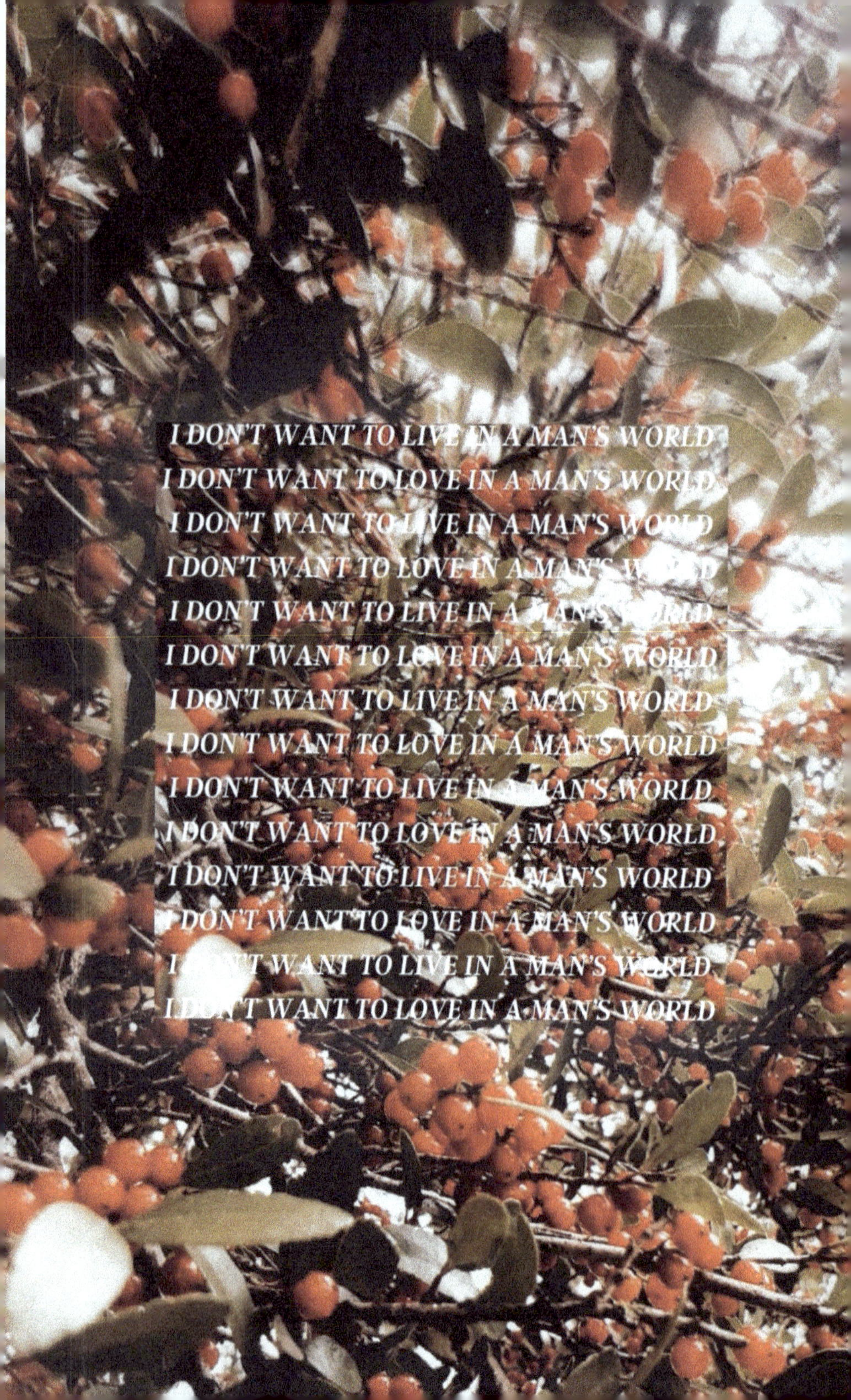
I DON'T WANT TO LIVE IN A MAN'S WORLD
I DON'T WANT TO LOVE IN A MAN'S WORLD
I DON'T WANT TO LIVE IN A MAN'S WORLD
I DON'T WANT TO LOVE IN A MAN'S WORLD
I DON'T WANT TO LIVE IN A MAN'S WORLD
I DON'T WANT TO LOVE IN A MAN'S WORLD
I DON'T WANT TO LIVE IN A MAN'S WORLD
I DON'T WANT TO LOVE IN A MAN'S WORLD
I DON'T WANT TO LIVE IN A MAN'S WORLD
I DON'T WANT TO LOVE IN A MAN'S WORLD
I DON'T WANT TO LIVE IN A MAN'S WORLD
I DON'T WANT TO LOVE IN A MAN'S WORLD
I DON'T WANT TO LIVE IN A MAN'S WORLD
I DON'T WANT TO LOVE IN A MAN'S WORLD

NIGHTS DISTURBED

i. I awoke deep within a dream again,
and when I flitted my eyes open,
it didn't feel real,
as if I was still detached from reality.
Through the morning,
the sky still a musty dark blue,
my voice felt distant as if
I was speaking through a rusted can
thrown across the room.

ii. Most nights I dream of the void,
an all-consuming darkness,
overwhelming but somehow calming.
When I stretch my arm out to reach into
the pure blackness,
I can feel the wisping pleasure of water
on my eager fingertips.

iii. I've dreamt about you several times
in these years,
and they've always been pleasant,
induced great bliss,
and made my heart very warm.
I wish I dreamt about you every night
but they are usually few and far between,
as if my mind does not want to
forget you
when I feel like I can finally move on.

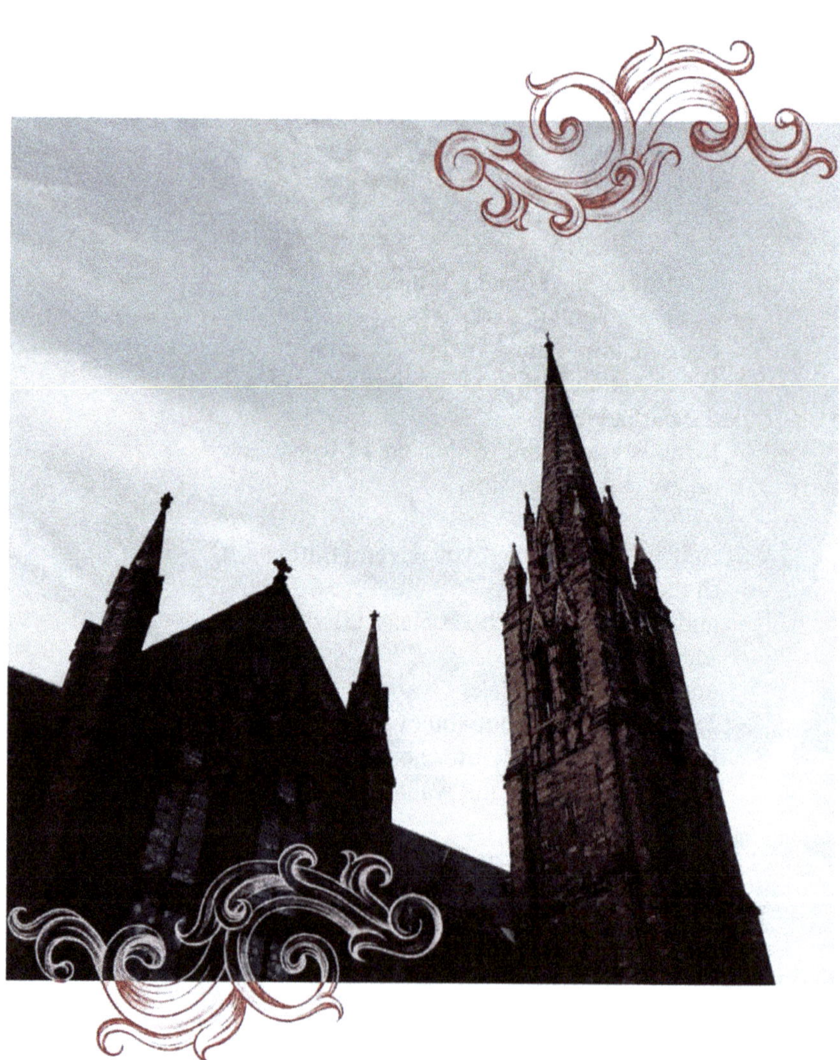

LIGHT OF THE STORM

My light, oh light.

A glittering shell
As if I were a mollusk;;
Beached and baking
In the summer Sun,
Pale with emptiness,
And shallow.

You came into my life
Quite suddenly,
Quite by mistake—
Feeding my empty shell
With wonder and
Aching curiosity.

My light, oh light—

I didn't see you as you were
Until the storm came & went,
First with water then with
Magnolias
Filling the quiet streets.

I awoke with a refilled heart
Beating, ravenous, and
bloody.

My light, oh my sweet light;;

I could not see you
for so long
Until the night you first
Haunted me
through the ether,
and the heinous dawn
The following morning.

Oh, to see you,
My dearest light,
In the dark depths
Of every passing storm.

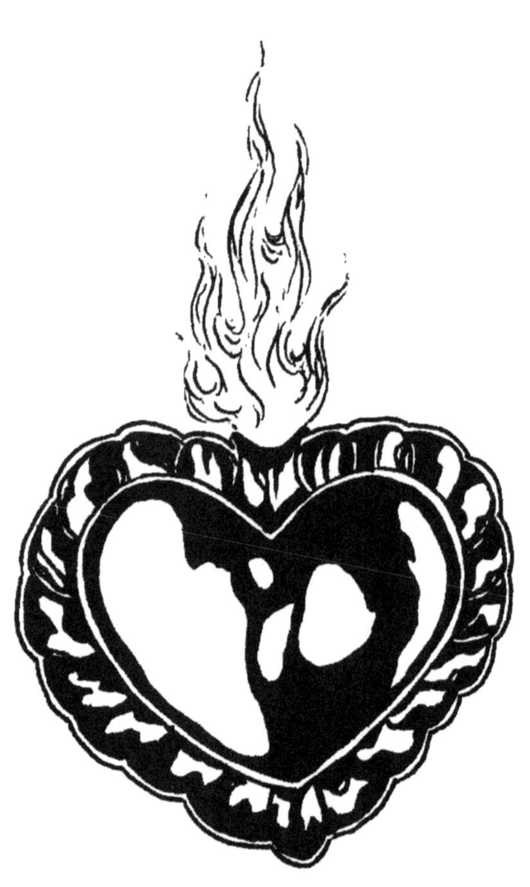

WITHIN MY SINEWS

My throat is arranged in violin strings
and *maybe* you don't know how to play.

If a guitar landed in my lap,
it would be like teaching my hands
how to speak a different language.

My notes come in brush strokes
that I know you have noticed,
you have seen,
because you told me so
and it warmed my slowly freezing heart.

You know my landscape is art nouveau,
and I know you are growing beautifully
because I can feel it just beneath
the surface of my skin.

If the cups fill up, give me a call—
I know they're for me and only me,
my king of the sea—
molting the body of the knight
whose charismatic vessel is a little emptier
than what I need.

I know you are growing
because I am growing too—
the cards had told me Temperance was near
and she sang me to sleep every night
telling me I needed to wait
because we are not who we are meant to be yet.

But dawn has finally arrived
and the Sun seems so much more delicate—
resembling everything I wished for ;;
I know the palm trees by the pool agree.

I have the key now and its
smooth figure feels good against my
burning fingertips.

Your energy is always rattling within my sinews,
And it's revitalizing – reinvigorating.

You gave me a piece of your life to
Put inside of my mouth

And I gave you a piece of me to put
Inside of your ears.

I can't wait to see how we
Change this year.

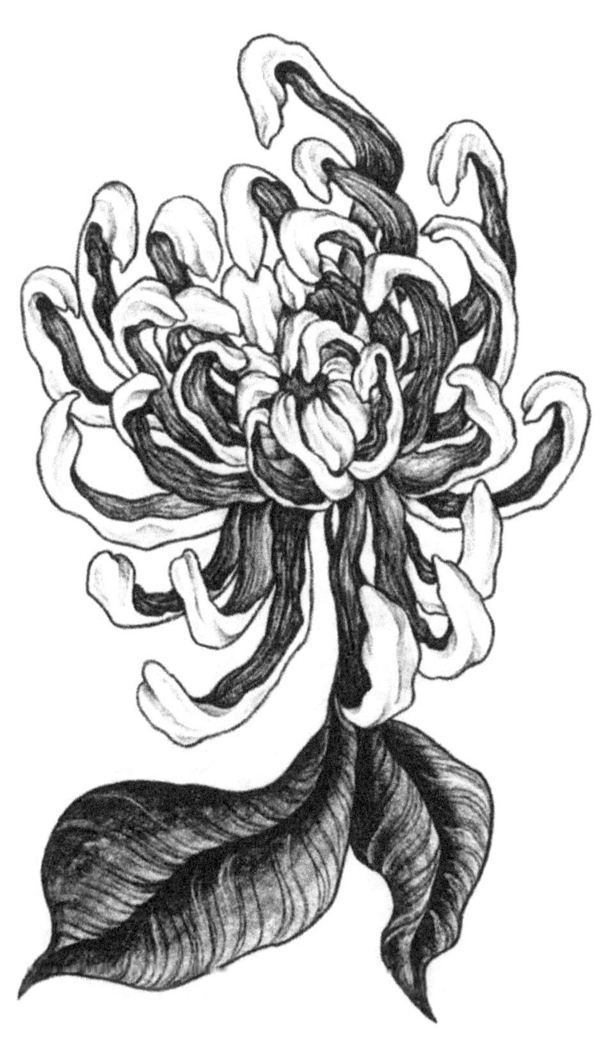

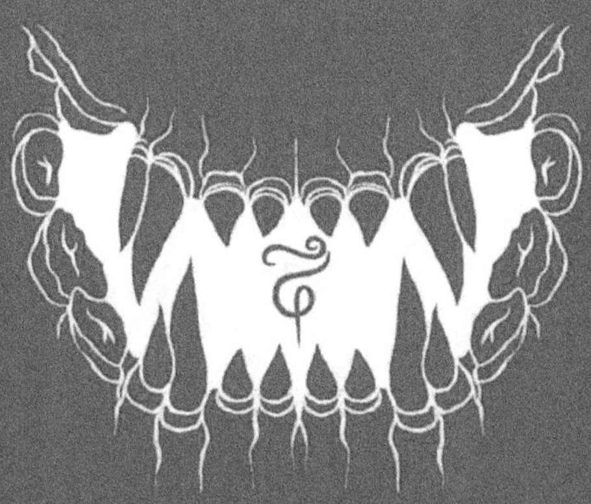

FERAL LOVE

- ii -

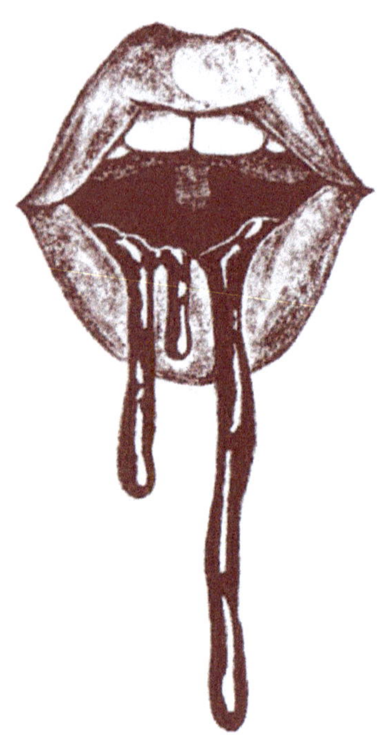

GARDEN OF EDEN

If I kissed you on your honey-sweetened lips,
would flowers grow in the negative space between our bodies?

And if you held my cold-bitten face
in your tender & warming hands,
would your blushing cheeks create dewdrops on the petals?

If *they* were to gaze into the garden,
would *they* see us through the dense brush?

And if I delicately wrapped my fingers around your shoulders,
and yours around my waist with such sensitivity,
would they sprout vines that would endlessly grow around us,
making us one for all eternity?

I know I would find the Garden of Eden inside your mouth
with the dancing tip of my tongue.

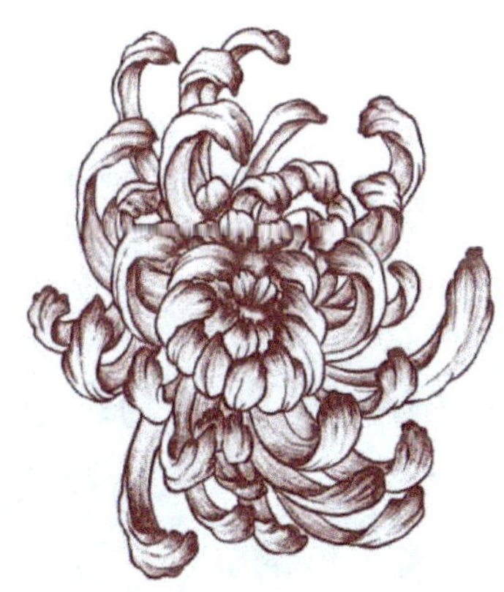

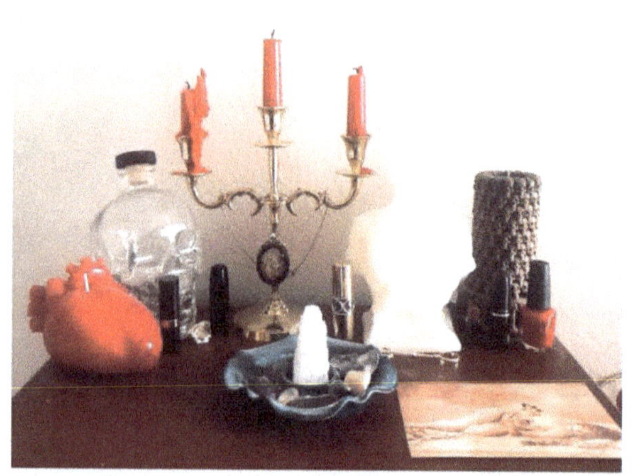

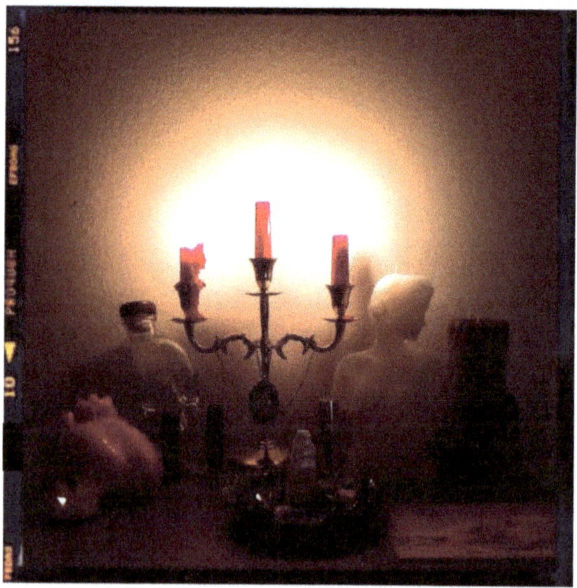

WITHIN THE CARDS LAY MY FATE

Temperance told me to be patient,
that the Star was on her way
to bring me the love I yearned for.
Though, she did not tell me
that the Tower had to fall first;;
though I think I knew.

I always feared the lightning storm,
but I didn't know you would be there
amongst the heavy rain
& that your laughter would be the thunder
off in the distance
drawing nearer with each passing moment.

I thought I could somehow bypass the storm,
that the Star would grant me your lips
under the cold of our old dusty city.

I didn't realize seeing you would be the storm
that brought my Tower down to Earth,
& I would be crushed under the rubble
Without You.

I HOPE TO SEE YOU IN HELL

I told the Moon about you first
through the bittersweet
blood-stained lips of the Dark Goddess.

She came rapping at my bedroom door
and whispered divine secrets
into my blushing and tender ears
on how to magnetize you.

And so twice every month,
as I studied the Night Mother and her
fluid phases,

I shifted my form into that of my
beautiful Dark Goddess ;;
my eyes transforming into those of the
asp that killed Cleopatra,

my teeth sharpened like some
Unaltered Beast,
ready to devour your beautiful, gleaming skin

and shred your temporal body
in a fit of ravenous pleasure—
like how a succubus fucks her victims into
a blissful death.

Because not being able to touch you
has made me unbelievably
feral for your love.

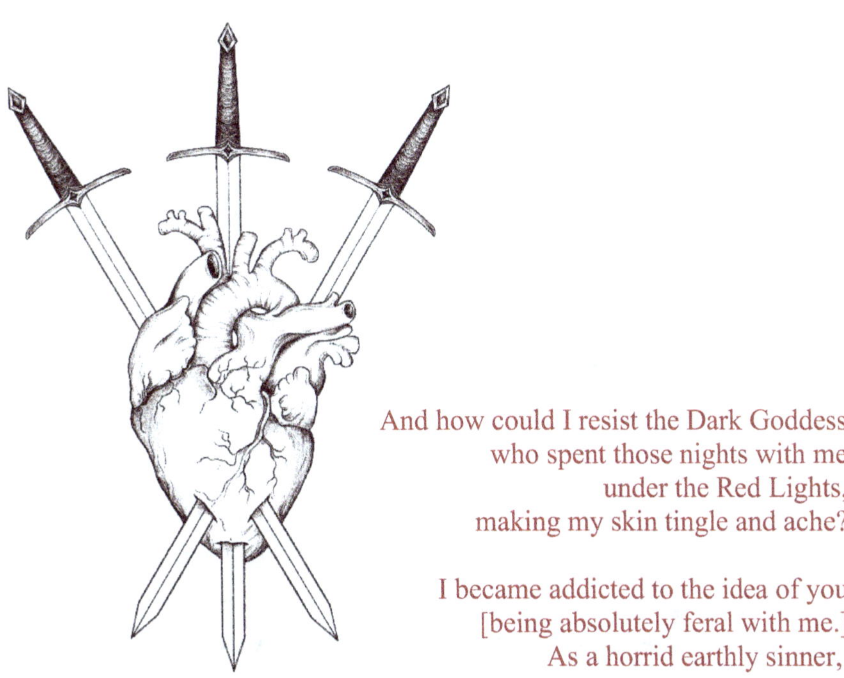

And how could I resist the Dark Goddess
who spent those nights with me
under the Red Lights,
making my skin tingle and ache?

I became addicted to the idea of you
[being absolutely feral with me.]
As a horrid earthly sinner,

I was not condemned to hell for an eternity
of torment, rather
appointed an infernal Queen of a ring
full of lost souls filled with a

certain lustful hunger
that would never be satiated.
And maybe you would be there,

pulsing and feverish,
on your knees praying up at me.
They would uncover from the
ashes of roses and their thorns

with our bones tangled together
as if we were some hellish ivy
curled up on itself.

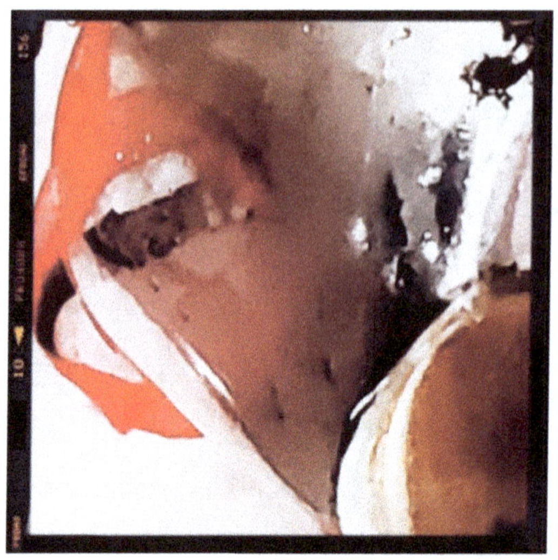

I ache with pleasure

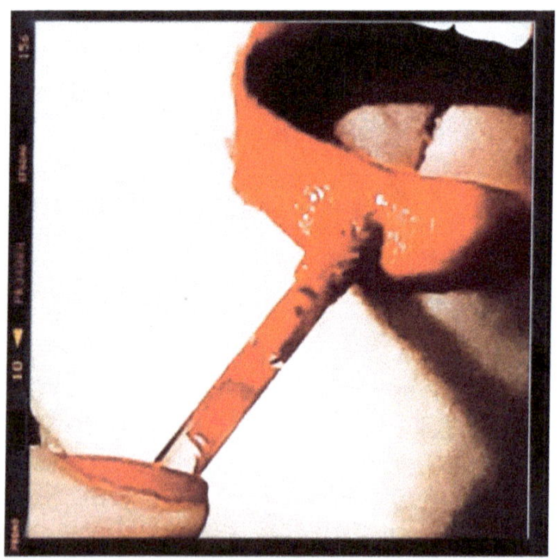

PREDATOR V. PREY

I dreamt of you
Clawing your way up
From the foot of my bed,
Anchoring yourself down into
The mattress with each
Of your fingertips,
With the eyes of a predator
Ready to devour its prey
As you pinned me
Underneath your warm body.

And how I usually *hate* being
The Prey,
But I would love to be yours—
To feel your teeth on my neck
With the warmth of
your love-drunken breath.
I would let you be my predator,
To feel I had been hunted
And conquered by you.

I'd fight back if you wanted me to,
Digging my nails into your skin
In a fit of bliss.

I have been keeping something hidden deep inside me for a long time, something that has been boiling and stewing. My blood courses red, my hands feel touchless, and I am worried that what has been burning my heart will soon bubble over into a tower moment.

And maybe this will reach the one who needs to read this, the energy I put into these words - god, I hope this finds you.

With every "end of the earth" and with every Lovers Tarot, I wonder where I am supposed to be and how I ended up here instead of there.

I am completely bound, 8 of swords.

And maybe casting spells is for the movies and reading poetry is for the hopeless romantics.

With hand in hand, and lips on lips, I'm delirious and stuck in a dream I hope to never really wake from, or at least hope my dream reflects my reality.

It was April in Boston, raining cats and dogs, magnolias hanging above me, and my dreams haunted by a figure I will never forget.

everyone is you
pushed out

and maybe I've been
calling you
home this whole time

1234

if you hear my
beckoning call in
your dreams, waking
to the color of my
eyes, know that I
heard your call first

ACTS OF DEVOTION

I soaked my hair in Rosemary to try to grow out the bald spots on my hairline
so You wouldn't notice them.

I plucked and shaved every inch of my body and moisturized with sweetness
in case You wanted a taste.

I meticulously manicured my nails and styled my hair
and dressed myself in appealing clothing

Because I'm out of practice in being attractive.
I don't even know what is attractive anymore.

Because before, I could just exist as a woman
and there would be a man kneeling down, kissing my feet.

But You are not at my feet,
worshiping me like I am Your God.

If I am writing a bible for You, I want You to play Your hymns for me.
Oh, how I want to be Your sensuous God,

to receive Your acts of devotion and offerings of
Blood in wine,
golden pearls,
silk and lace,
of long and steady kisses tracing the frame of my body.

Oh, how I wish to be the altar that You pray at
when the Moon isn't watching.

Instead, in some sick and cruel way,
You are my God,

To whom I devote my tears to, my intimacy to, my creations to.
You are who I devote my beauty to,

Sacrifice my rituals for.
It's cruel that You do not worship me

like I worship You.

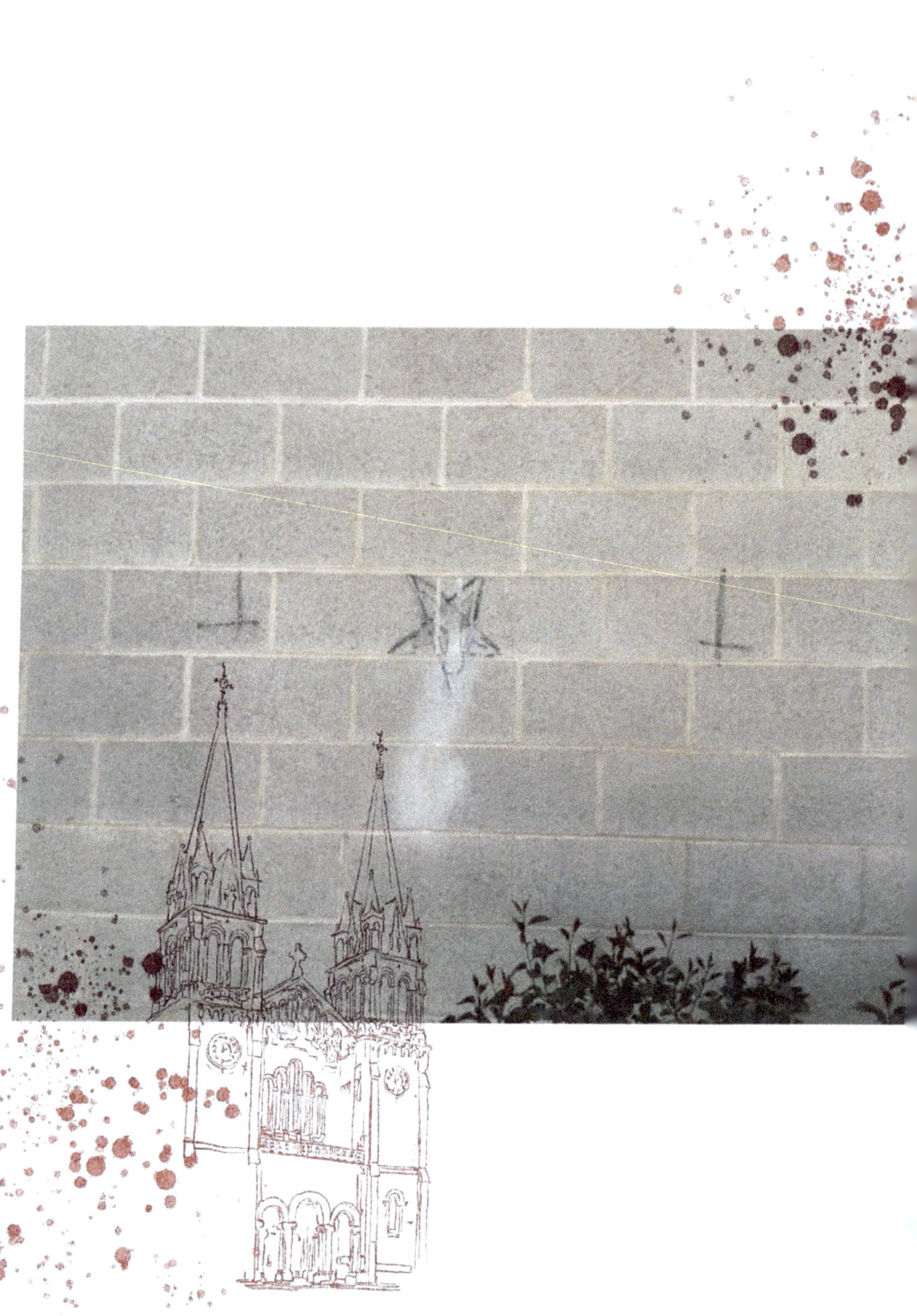

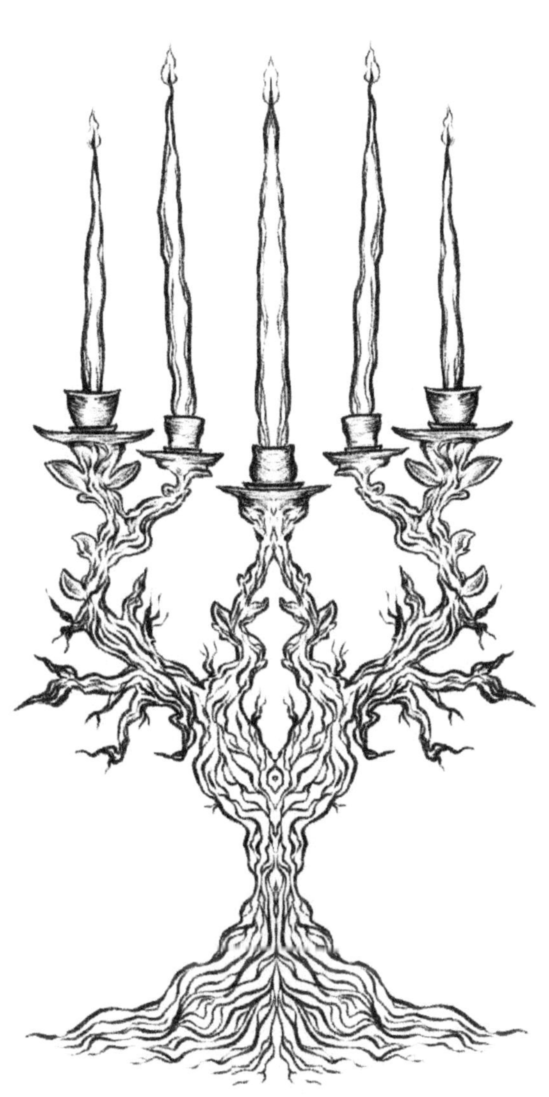

INCUBATOR

I exist as a crystalized brain
inside of a woman-body;
and that doesn't really mean much,

it just means that my blood
is sweet like candied rose petals
and cinnamon sticks

and vanilla bean,
but I have so much of it
that it feels like a curse.

And whenever I bleed
and *bleed* and *bleed* and *bleed*,
I can feel Gaia crying for me,

with me,
as the pain swells from my womb,
a womb I will never use.

And oh, how I have envisioned
forcing a serrated spoon up
into the cavern between my thighs to

swivel and gut and yank
that accursed womb from my body.
How I cry and scream for

pure hatred of an incubator I'm
forced to have.
How I wish sometimes to mutilate

my insides and sew the door shut—
    how I wish to cut off my breasts
        and throw them to the dogs

so that other men may never look at me.
    And I could massacre my woman-body
        all I want but

I know that some man out there
    would find some way
        to violate me.

DAUGHTER OF LILITH

What is the honest difference between the bible and a witch's grimoire? // One contains the secrets on how to manifest your desires and the other makes you fear your only earthly existence. // I wrote succinct notes in mine about red candle wax on unsuspecting flesh and dried roses mixed with the ashes of old lovers. // I'm a witch because I don't fear an imaginary omnipotent force and have generously placed the power back into my own hands. // It all means the same thing, though. // Daughter of Lilith born on Earth with a serpent's tongue and addicting eyes so divine – *man eater*. // And how would anyone know if these are my spells or the soaking letters of a tattered heart? // Shaken, never stirred. Over ice? // My bones were forged from gold, but my blood remains very human. // Oh, to be inhumanly human. // I have always believed, in some cruel way, that I was born to be The Muse – inspiring and provocative, where songs would be written about me, characters in books and movies even. // Where I would inspire devilish creation related to lust & heartbreak, longing & beauty. // Does that idea diminish me as a creatrix? Am I ultimately devaluing all of my work? // Or does that mean I control both sides of the same coin – to have my own opulent creations while also creating through the minds and hands of others?

Have you written a song about me, my beloved? What does it taste like when you sing it to yourself in your darkened bedroom? Does it give you immense pleasure to have that creation that is ultimately mine?

Can you hear my serpent tongue hissing when you turn out all the lights?

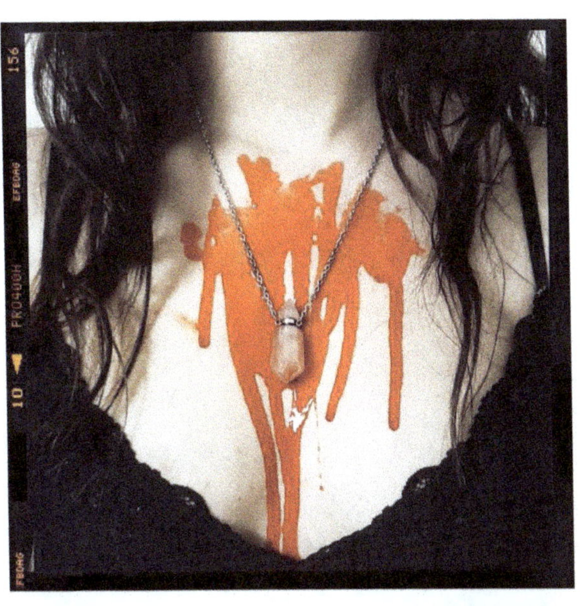

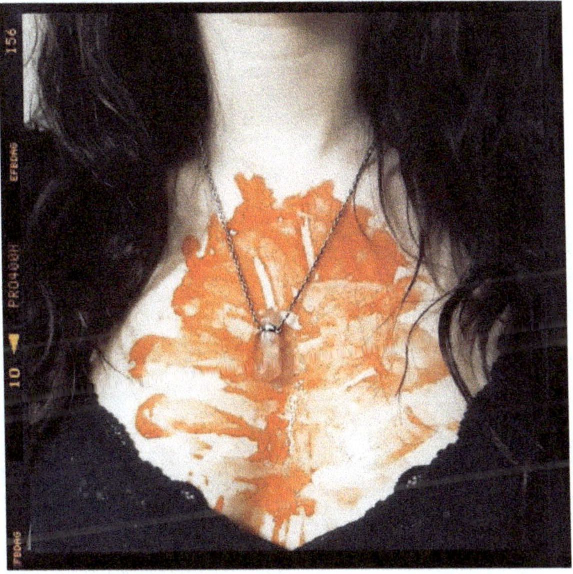

SKYCLAD

I've thought of dancing skyclad
With the Devil himself,
If damnation was my fate anyway—

Though,
I don't think a man would
Be able to empathize with me

And my vehement female rage.
I would dance skyclad with the Devil,
Though I think Lilith would

Roll her serpent eyes.
If the Devil himself touched my
Bare human flesh under

The light of the silver Moon,
His demonic hands might burn
As his touch is unwanted.

If he were to scoff at my
Humanly flaws,
Does that mean the Devil himself

Exists in every earthly man?
If God created man,
Does that also make him

A raging misogynist?
If I stood skyclad
In front of an earthly man,

And he did not pick me apart
But rather
Cherish my beauty and

Worship my divinity,
Does that mean he has
Accepted his mother's blood?

If I was born skyclad
Before God and the Devil
Into a world where

Men hate everything women are,
Then how am I supposed
To find one who truly loves me?

One who will cherish my beauty
And worship my divinity?

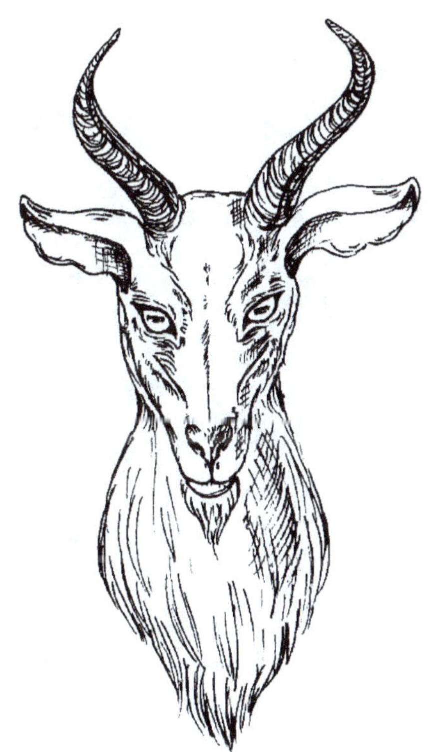

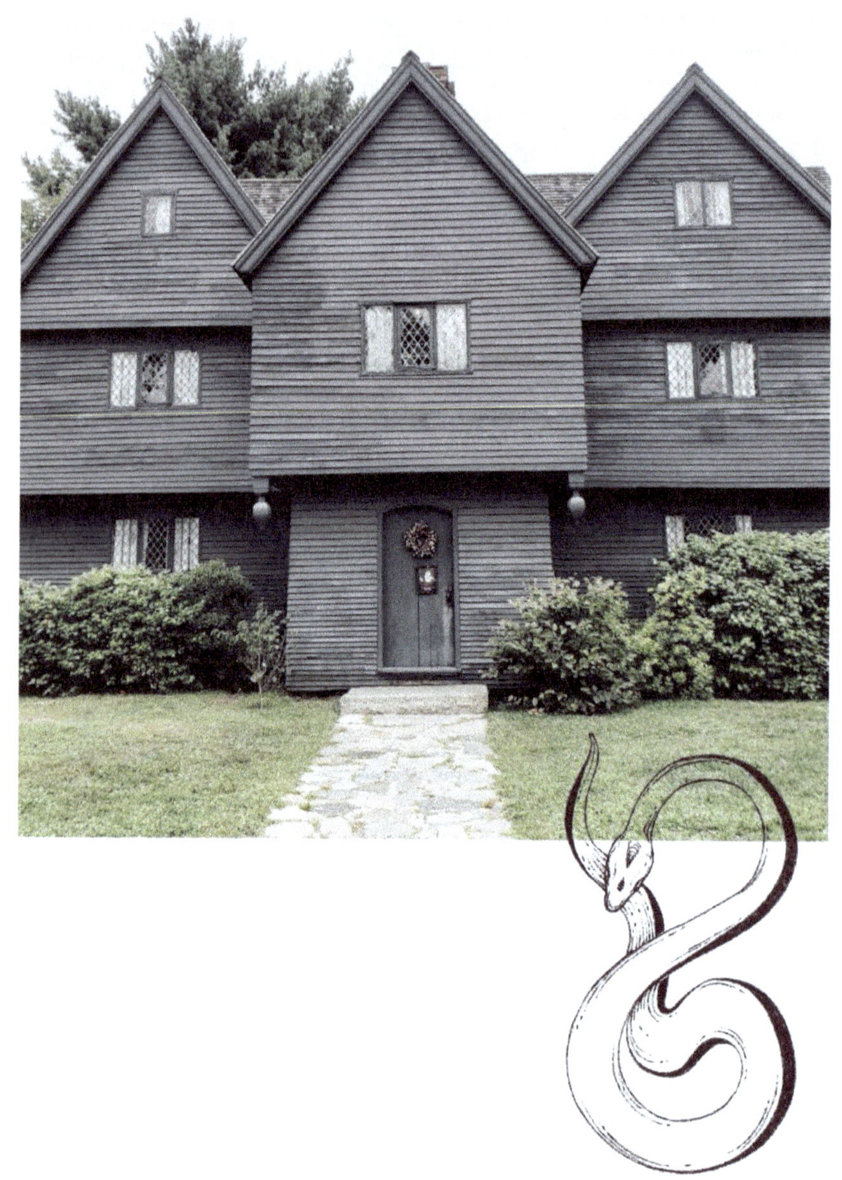

WHAT YOU NEED

Begin again with whispers into the ether—
          little whisper secrets for your burning ears,
and may your lips only be kissed ;;
          sweetly, tenderly, lovingly, passionately ;;
by mine.

Can you hear in my distant voice how I ache?
          I know I have said it a million times—
repeated under my trembling breath,
          going unheard, unnoticed.

Have you ever wondered the taste of my
          collar bone on your lips?
Send chills down my spine and an
          undeniable warmth to my sacral.

Begin again with your hand in mine—
          as if I am all you need in this life ;;
and maybe I am what you need—

your oxygen—
          so breathe me in,
my Man from Mars.

EARTHQUAKE BOY

I felt you in my spine today
and I'm not *exactly* sure why.

I think underneath all the flesh and blood;
the tissues and fat and veins and

fucking whatever human nonsense,
bones feel every earthquake,

and I think I felt you quaking,
my trembling boy.

And on the spire hung another fresh breath,
fogging mirrors and stoking fires,

as if the layers couldn't keep you warm—
my shivering, shaking, quaking, trembling little boy.

Put on your coat before the snow falls,
even if the sun is blazing.

Because my fingertips froze into icicles
but my bones tell me you're still earth-quaking.

The liquor and the sugar won't warm your blood—
nothing will but the fire that rages on inside of me.

If my heart was set ablaze,
then how is it not completely charred?

And do you find it degrading
when I call you "boy"?

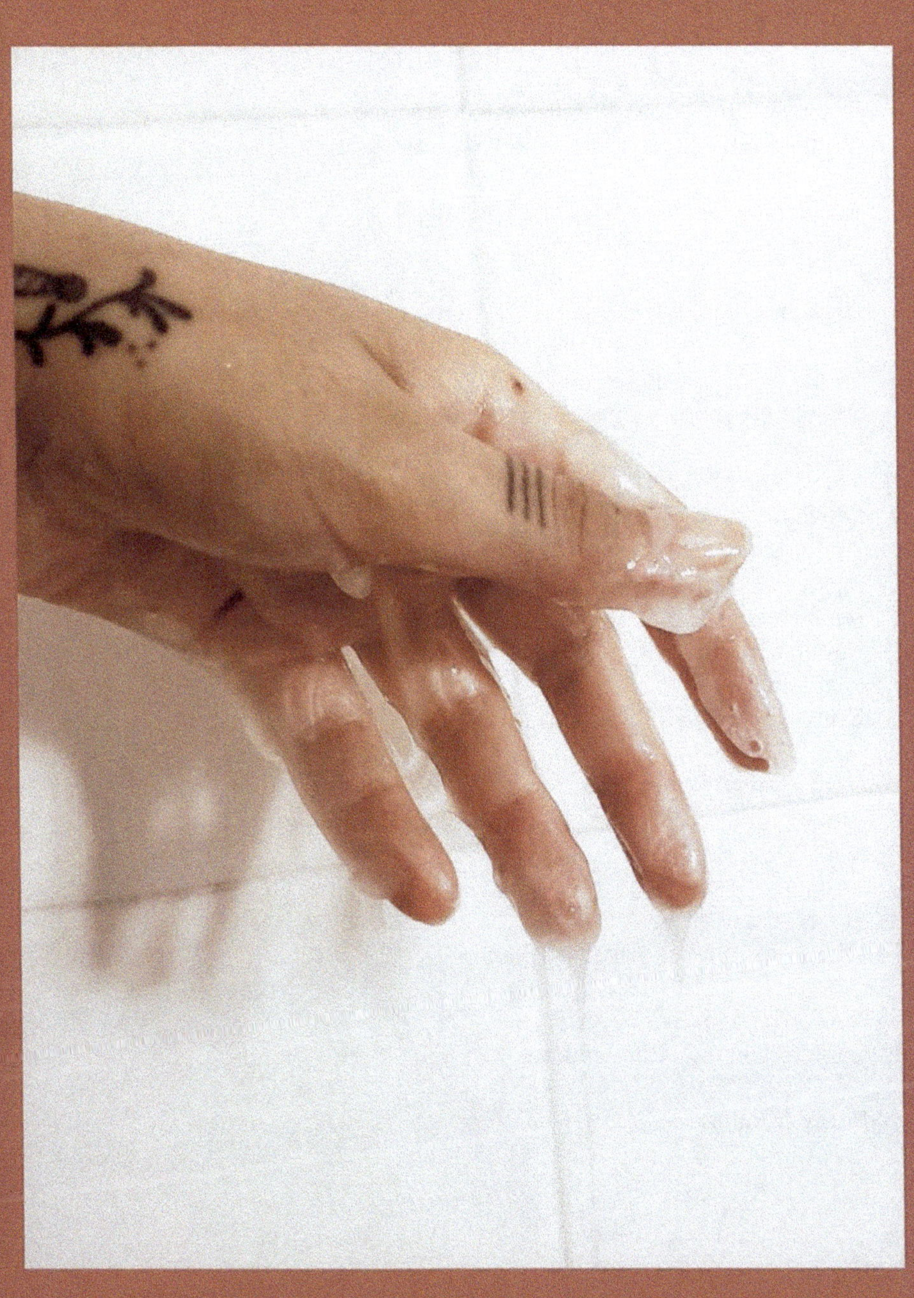

PURITY

I think I love the disgusting ::
The gross, the uncomfortable, the degrading,
With specific exceptions.

Curated human grossness is fascinating—
Warm seed hitting my bare skin,

(though sometimes the smell makes me gag.)

Or the specific way sex smells in a car ;;
Absolutely mortifying and animalistic.

I love how my spit feels running
Down my pink fingertips,
And I've decided I would absolutely

(*enthusiastically*) ask you to
Spit in my mouth,

Knowing full well it might taste like

Your sweet timidity.
I love biting off the peeling skin

From my fingers and leaving
The pieces everywhere.
I think love makes grossness pure,

Pure and clean and angelic.
Orifices leaking clear and clean

Purity from divine lust.

Eggs and eyes are all the same,
Dripping in saliva and sweat.

If your skin is salty,
I want to lick it clean ;;
Pure and clean and angelic—

Glowing beautifully in the moonlight.
Raised skin and drawn blood

From my little brittle fingernails.

Intertwined bodies coated in
Combined salty sweat

As our mixed odors create the most
Decadent perfume.
I'll huff your unbathed skin like it

Was my preferred drug—
Pheromones ;;

With biting and sucking and tugging

To make us
Pure and clean and angelic.

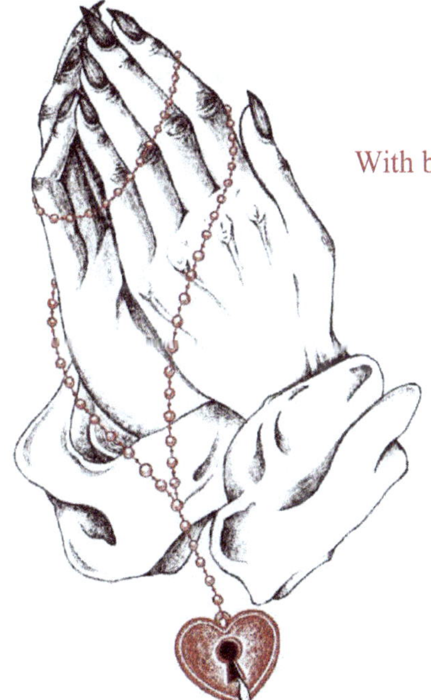

MESSAGES FOR THOSE WHO NEED THEM

A woman with a butterfly between her eyes

Fire igniting from flowing air

Fragments of something lost soon to be found

Tears from sinful play, howling bitterly into the midnight moon

THE TOWER

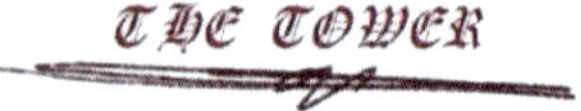

Inspiration found in different corners

The mind's eye awakens a dusty copper pink

A door closes – a new one opens before you, what do you see?

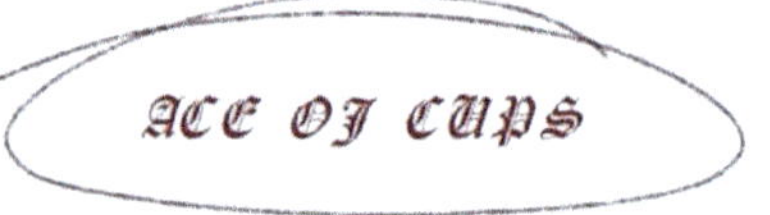

ACE OF CUPS

A sun on your fingertips

An instrument whistling in the wind

Love found in unexpected places

1111

777

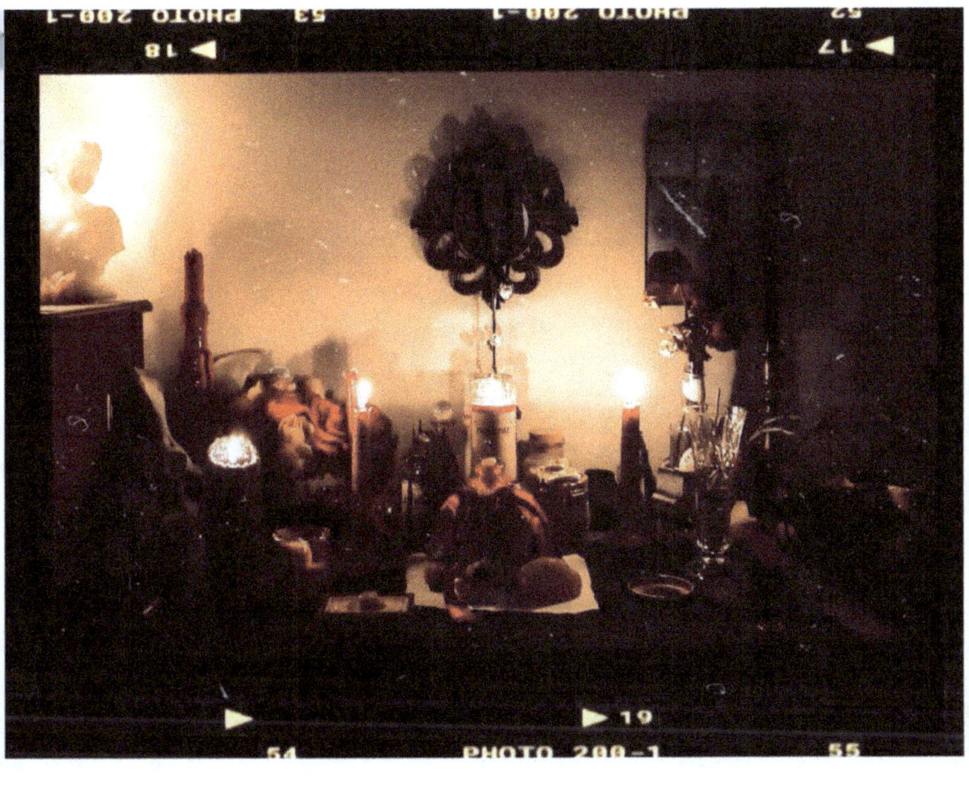

DIVINE FEMALE RAGE

Why does my heart cry
When it's all just blood?
I feel it pulsing in my
Aching veins—
Something excruciating
And vile.

In what Universe does it
Make any crumb of sense
For me to be this
Fucking angry *constantly*?

So angry that blood
Pours out from every
Orifice on my exposed body?

And sometimes rage feels like
My only true talent
As I'm unreasonably good
At being utterly demonic
And uncontrollable.

My existence is gore,
My joints, white from clenching
My face, red with ichor.

Who am I without my
Detestable rage?

Who am I if
There isn't someone out there

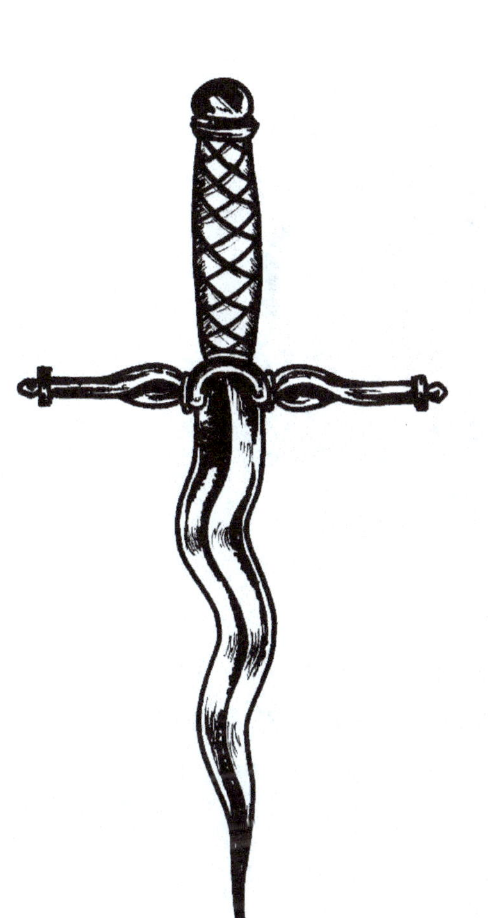

With the impurest intentions
Telling me I have
Outstanding anger issues?

Who am I if
There's isn't some
Arrogant man
Telling me I'm always
Too negative?

As if they've even
Had the misfortune
Of walking in my
Blood-flooded shoes.

As if I don't exist purely
Out of spite and vengeance.

How easy is it
To be a nightmare,
A night terror?
And can I be yours?

Maybe now you will dream
Of me – divine beauty,
Devouring your damp flesh
And then disintegrating
Into a horrid gory pile
Of my own flesh and blood
Mixed with yours.
Delicious.

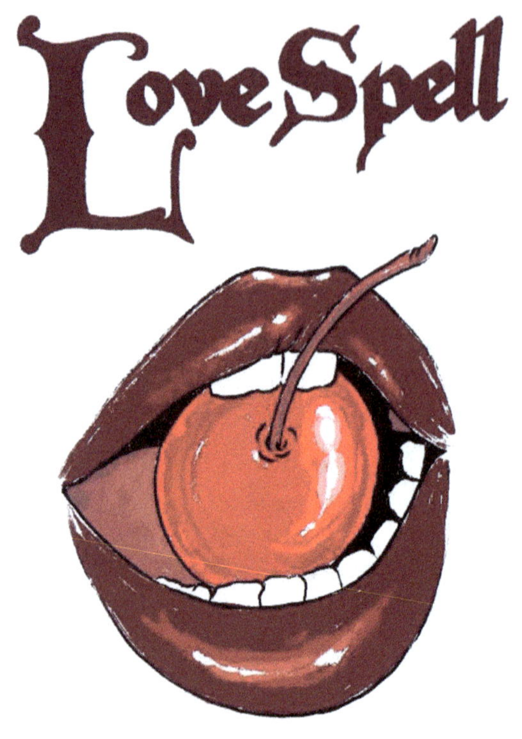

tying a knot in a cherry stem with your tongue
is a seduction spell, definitely.

we have all dabbled in witchcraft.
do not deny your birthright.

A LOVE SPELL TO ATTRACT [*****]

Ingredients:
(herbs can be dried or fresh)

- red rose petals
- lavender buds
- crushed cinnamon stick
- chamomile flowers
- white cyclamen flower
- rose hips
- hibiscus
- lemon balm
- orange peel
- jasmine buds
- pink Himalayan salt
- witch's black salt
- love oil of your choosing
- red candle, any size

If I close my eyes and think about you hard enough, you become real. / And within myself, the pink light grows and swells beyond the capacity of my trembling chamber. / Bones and Flesh melt away as I become one with the pink light emanating from my heart-center. / Suddenly, I am merging with the cosmos above me – a daughter of the Universe. / Breathing ceases to exist – I am gently afloat among my sister stars and they use their twinkling fingertips to graze my chilled skin – I am glitter and needles. / You are real in my cerebral embrace ; may our energies dance for all eternity – unity. /

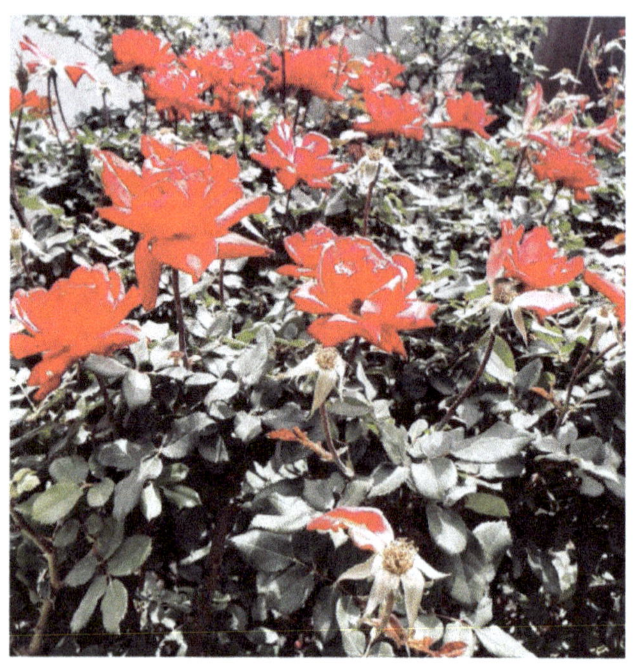

THE GARDEN OF LILITH

I saw you at the corner gates // through the thorny vines of rose bushes // holding the malum malus for me // where the blissful evil in our truth // will be revealed. // The serpent awakens at my breast // hungry for divine knowledge, // the throbbing lamb's heart at // our combined core. // I speak your name as if it were the first sound in existence // its sweet taste an eternal song. // Devour me with your god-given teeth // I know she is watching from the drifting storm over us. // The lightning – my sharp inhalation // as you draw my blood onto your tongue. // The thunder – your booming exhalation // as you grow addicted to the taste. // All we do is moan and blush because // the Sun's fire is what's most familiar. // And it's strange how quickly I move these days // as nothing outside our darkened // and lustful safe-haven // feels the least bit real. // If my dreams are flashing within my reality, // maybe my mental clarity is dwindling // or I'm returning to some demonic form // I'm meant to be in; // and I guess it's refreshing // to see you there too, // with your fiery forked tongue // and matching serpent eyes.

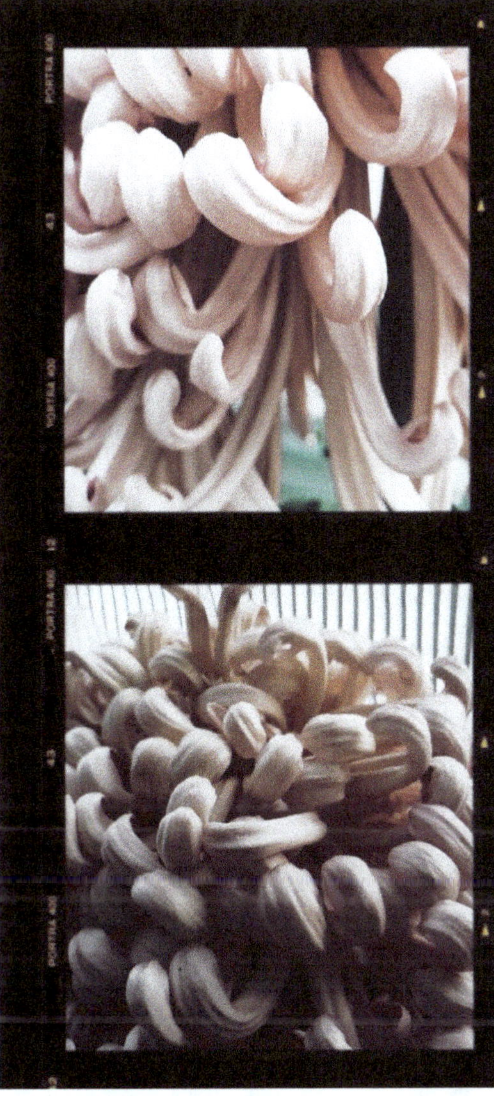

INTERMISSION - STONE FRUITS FOR THOUGHT

I've been thinking about the Universe for as long as I can remember.
It's amazing how what seems to be infinite is constantly expanding—
meaning Infinity is always getting bigger.
Infinite possibilities are growing in numbers.
How can we say,
with our limited
(pathetic)
human senses what is real/possible and what isn't when every single day,
Infinity grows bigger?

Are we truly here by mere chance or is there a reason for everything?
If you were put on this earth
(a tiny, microscopic speck in the face of the Universe)
with me, and I with you,
and our very Universe
(absolute Infinity)
is always expanding,
then why can't I
(insignificant)
tell you
(also insignificant)
with my very own voice
(small insignificant noise)
how I truly feel
(a tiny blip in the history of the Universe)?

I'm not sure why we place such importance
on things that are truly meaningless and
purposefully spend our only lives suffering for no good reason
(capitalism, religion, media, beauty standards, politics).

If anything, I was meant to lie naked in a field of flowers
eating stone fruits with you under the beautiful Sun.

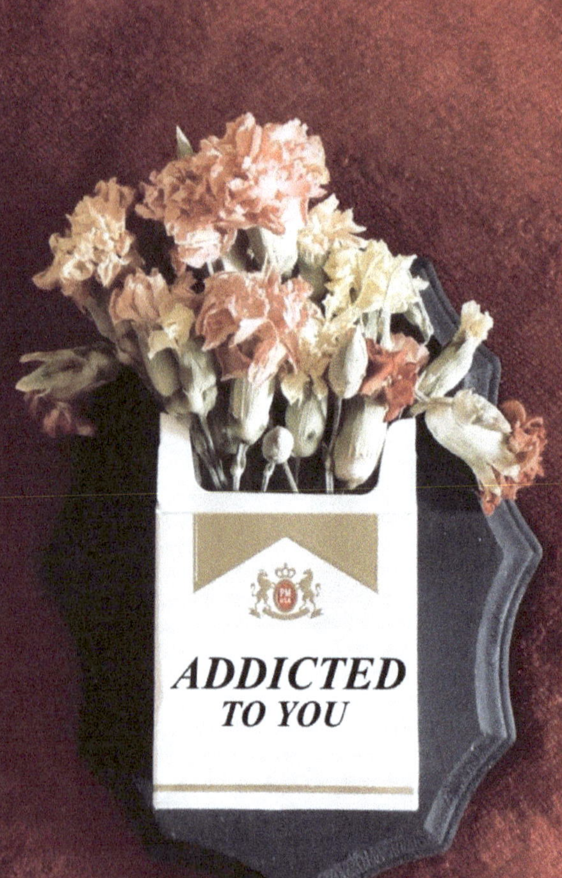
ADDICTED
TO YOU

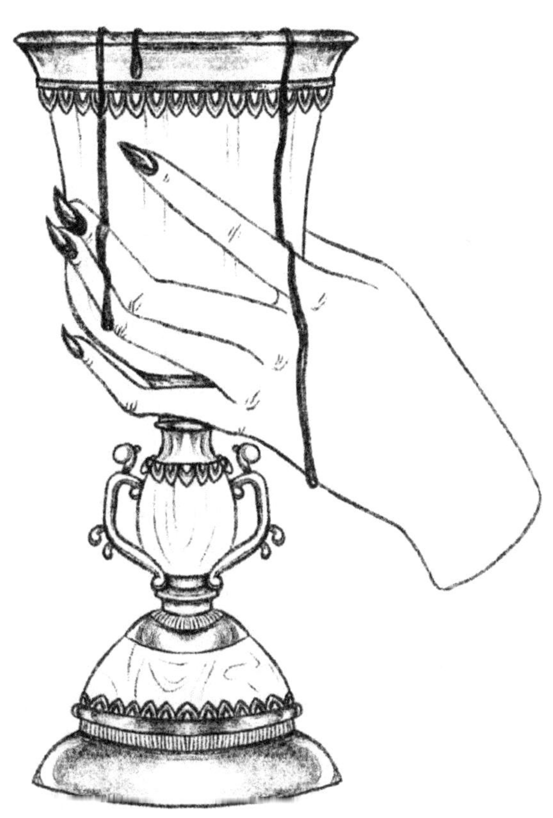

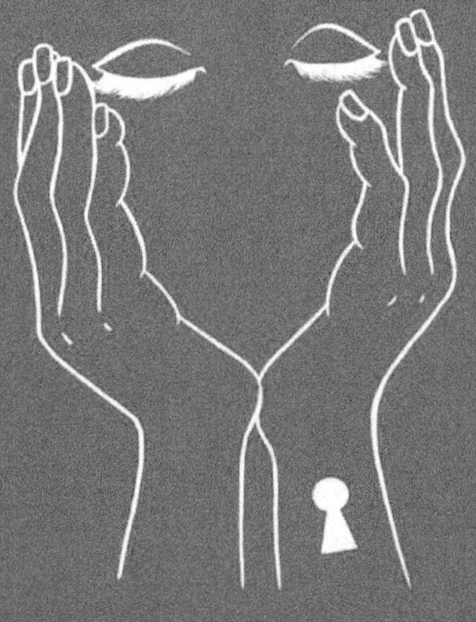

STARGIRL

- iii -

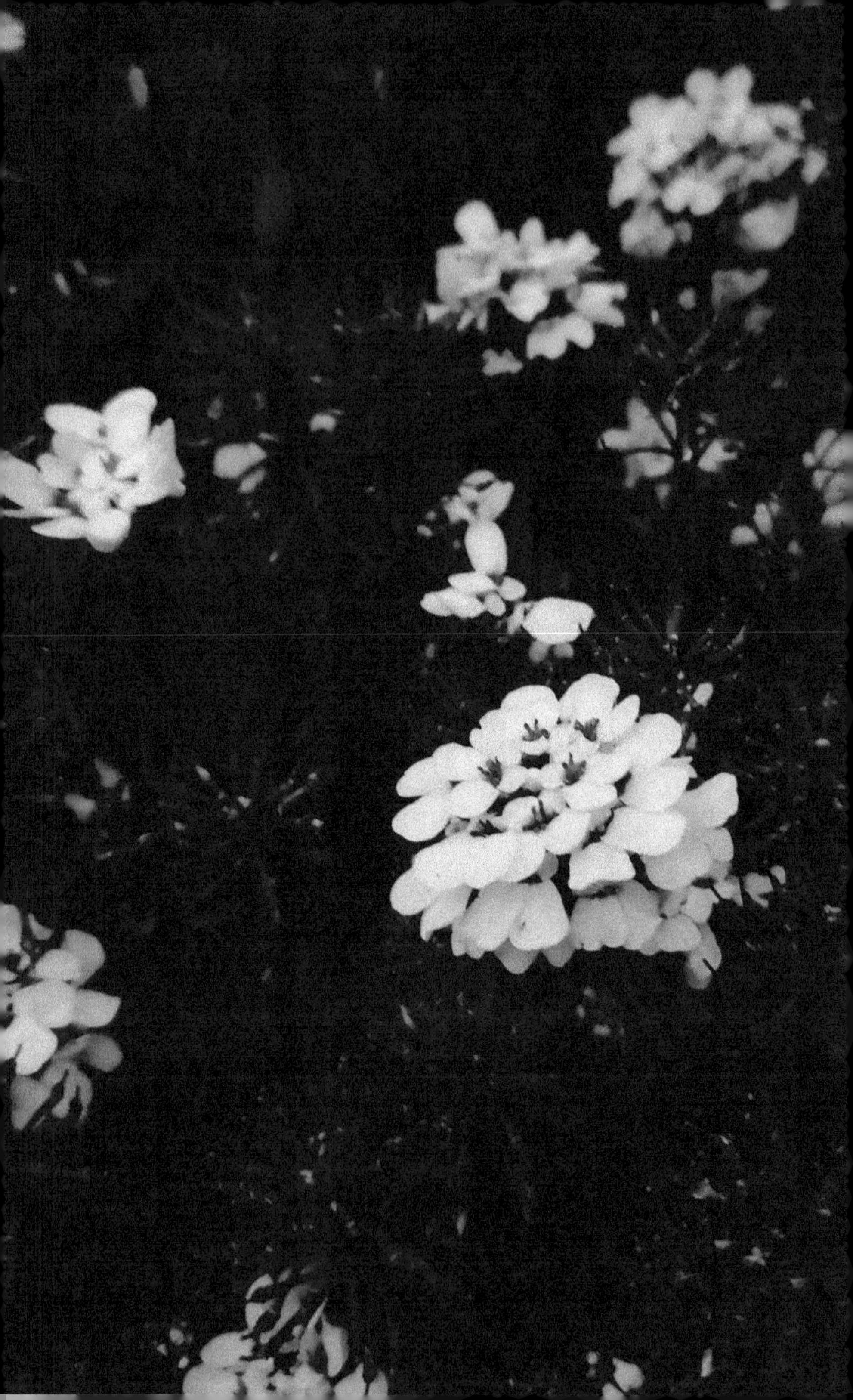

THE STARS OF DAWN

When I think of you,
I twinkle and glisten like
The Stars of Dawn ;;
and the blood rushes to my

Lips & cheeks
bringing the Sun to my face
and a bursting fire to my thighs
that I know you will only stoke
rather than douse.

How the fire within my body
makes me crave your touch.
How I ache for your heavy breathing
on my exposed neck.

Beneath all the little nuances,
I know that when I think of you,
my heart sings and cries to
The Stars of Dawn.

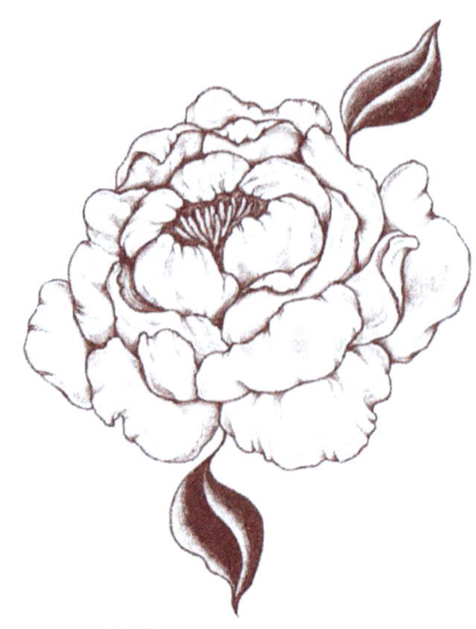

SOMEDAY WINTER WILL BE OURS

We will dance
In the rain
Like we have nothing to lose.

Maybe you will fumble
And I'll giggle
But you won't blush or hide.

You might gaze into my eyes
And fall into their light,
Maybe even gasp
At what you might find.

I think we will fall in love
Under the glistening stars
Hidden amongst the winter trees—

And perhaps you will kiss me
Because you finally realized
That we have nothing to lose.

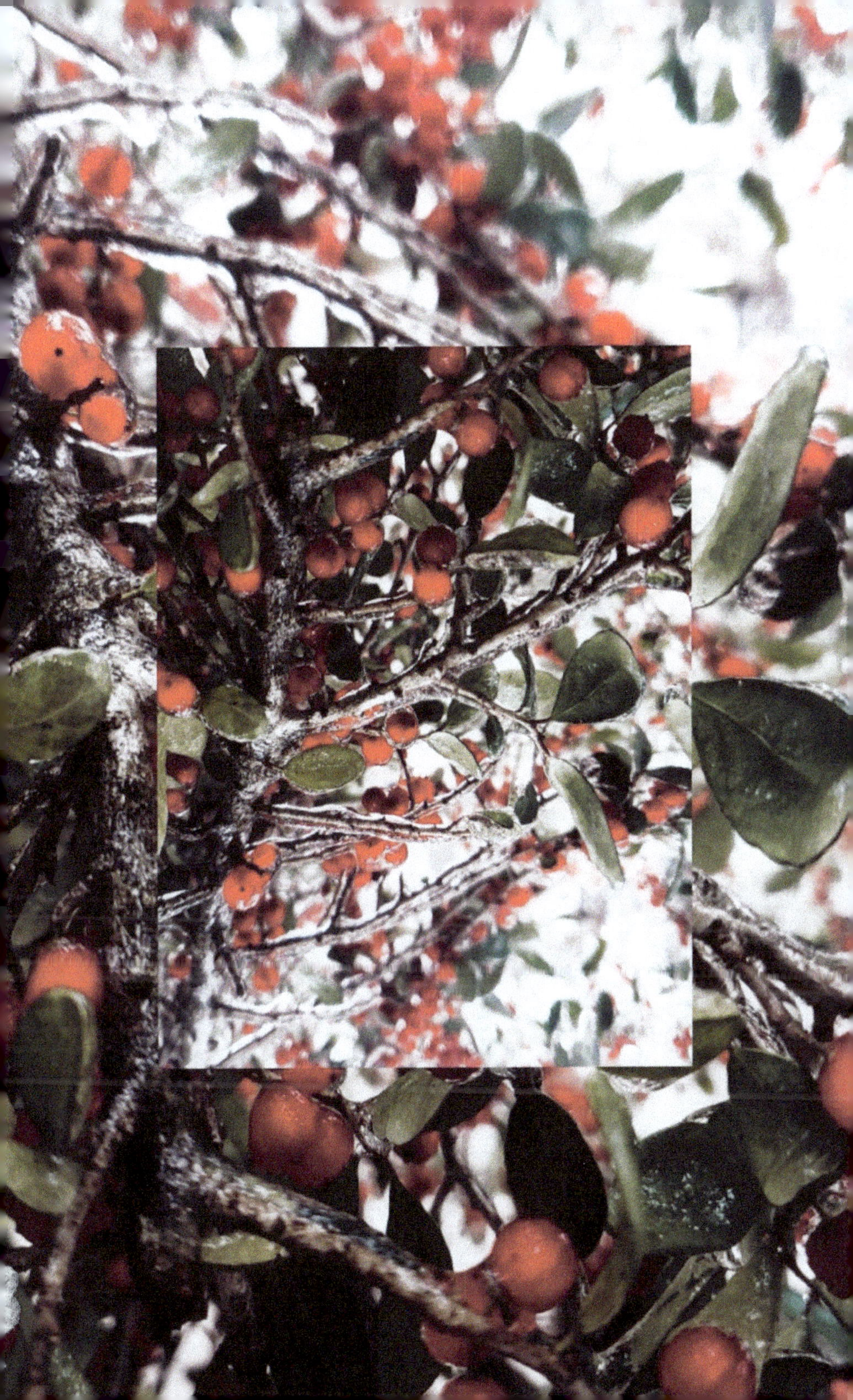

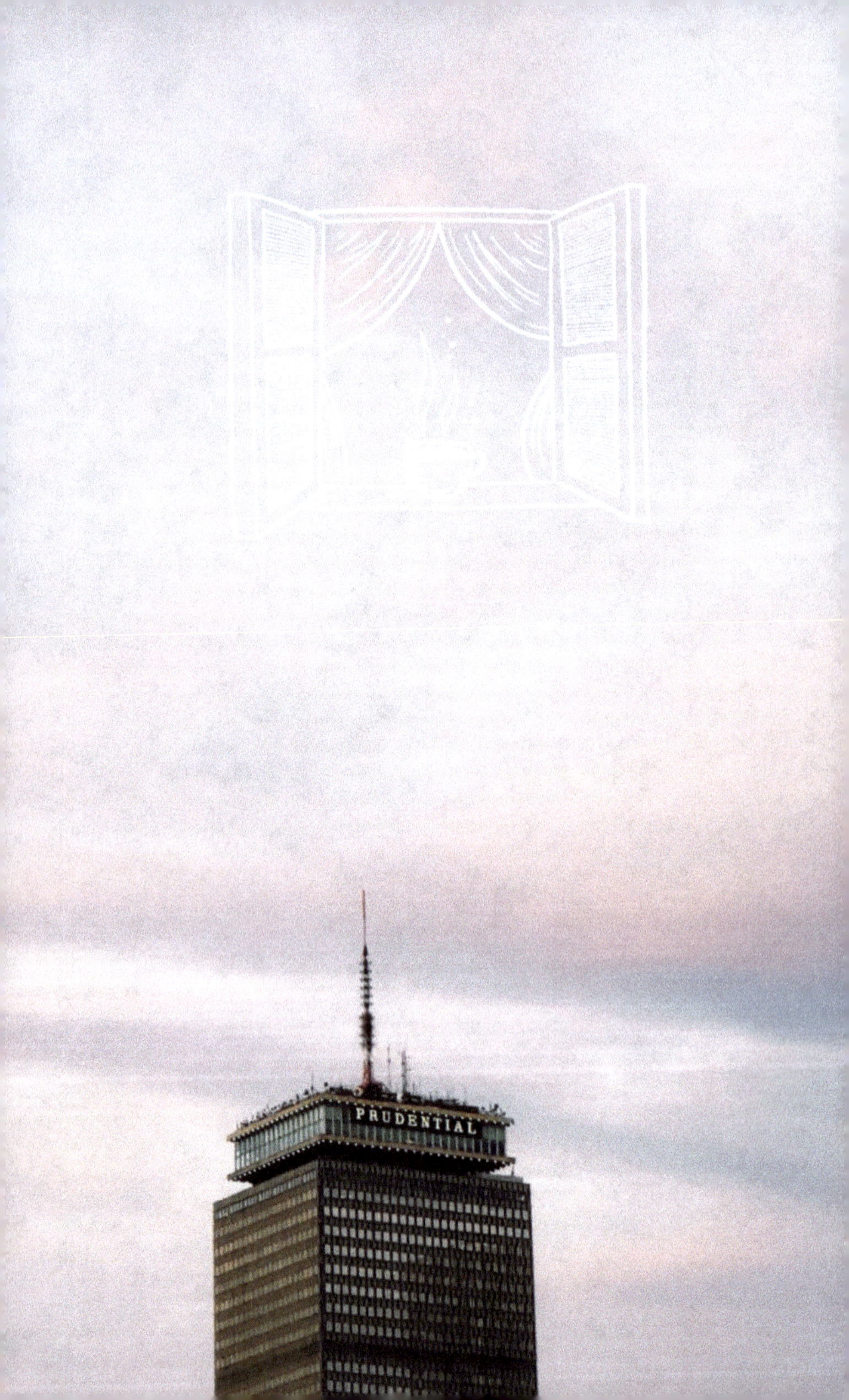
PRUDENTIAL

MAN FROM MARS

I hope I whispered the right words into your unsteady & racing mind.
I hope I filled your chest with fiery confidence – because you looked so radiant and beautiful.
I hope I made you smile in a way you will never forget ,,
And keep you awake with blissful thoughts of me.
I hope my words of the cosmos will forever echo in your sweet, curious, unsteady & racing mind.
I hope I changed your perspective to include me and mine.

Because your beautiful words filled my heart with infernal love.
I knew for the first time that you had really seen me.
Your words will always make my heart fidget and blush.
You made me beam and laugh in a way I never have before.

Oh, my beautiful Martian Man, I am forever your loving Venusian Muse.

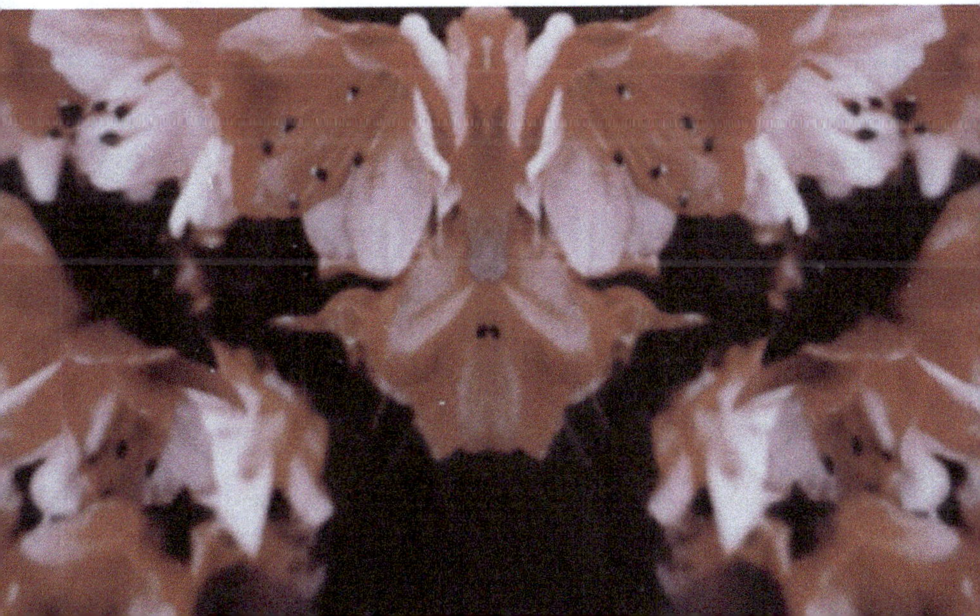

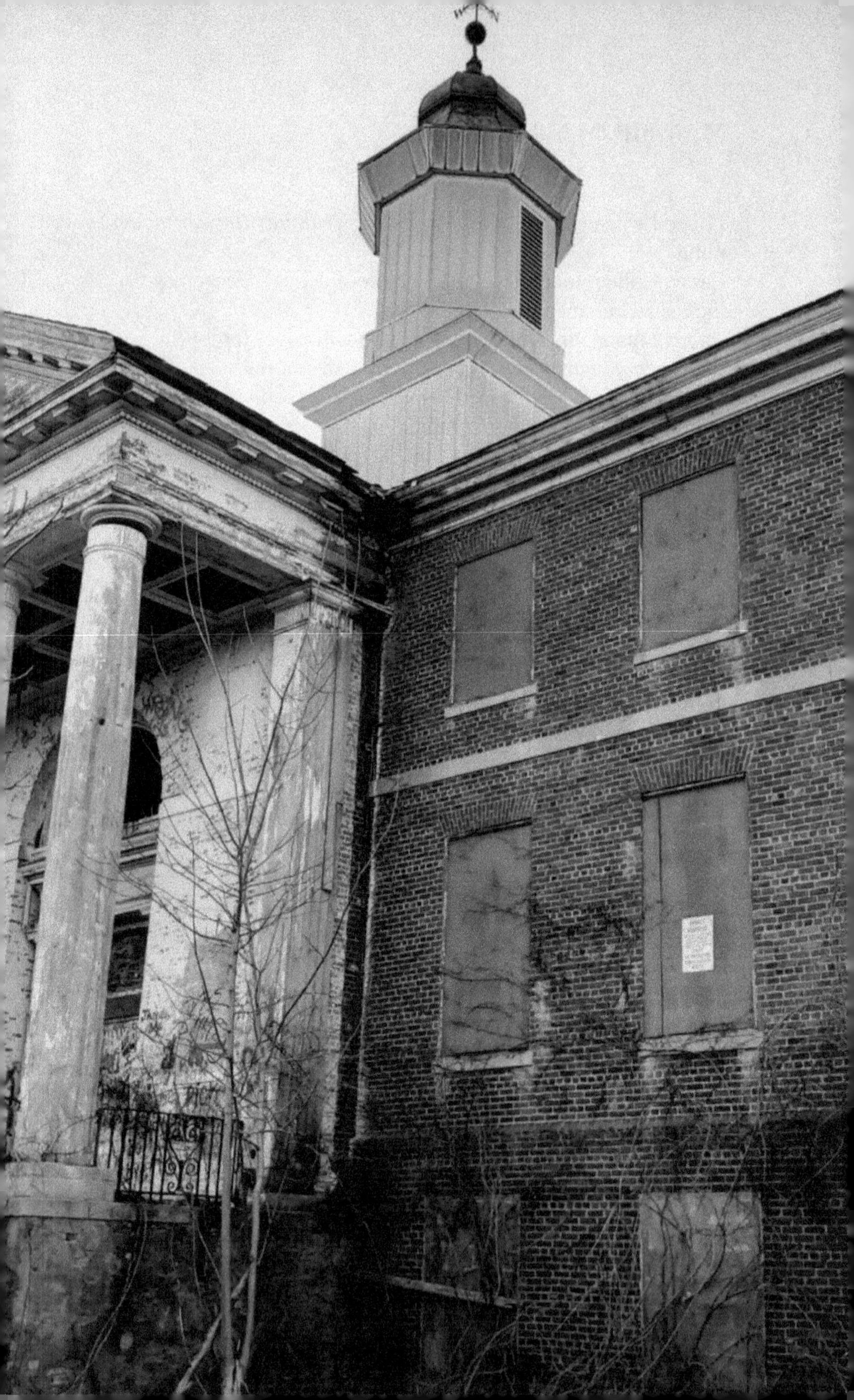

THE WILLOW TREE

I think before I was human
I might have been a towering willow tree
With full and delicate hanging tendrils,
Brushing my bittersweet leaves on
Passersby to make them feel safe
In my shade.

And although I'm sure my roots were firmly
Planted in the untainted soil,
I must have been at the mercy of
The unrelenting tempest,
Knocking my sturdy core to meet the earth,
With those roots I was so proud of
Shining bright in the watchful Sun.

With passing years,
The gentle and caring nature of that
Willow tree must have carried over
Within me,
As I crave to nurture and heal as
A tree would, with security & stability.

And when I see you clenching nervously,
Stiff as a board a sober man,
I only wish to graze my fingertips,
Like my delicate, leafy tendrils,
Against the skin of your face,
Dragging longingly through your hair
To make you feel safe and peaceful
In my shade.

ST. JAMES INFIRMARY BLUES

My darling dearest,
my beloved angel,

I will see you at
St. James Infirmary.

With your sweet and
cold body
stretched out on a

long white table,
lips blue and still.

How I prayed the kisses
I sent through the ether

Would keep those
beautiful lips
Red and warm.

When I die,
I want to be buried next

To the Atlantic
And I hope you will meet me

By the Bay
With the leaves a
crimson red

And the rain
beginning to ice.
And may your lips
blue mine

With a sweet and
gentle kiss.
And may we chant our

Unfinished business into
The unsteady air.

Take my hand,
Darling apparition,

As we glide into the water—
To be two crimson leaves

Drifting off on the surface
Of the blue sea.

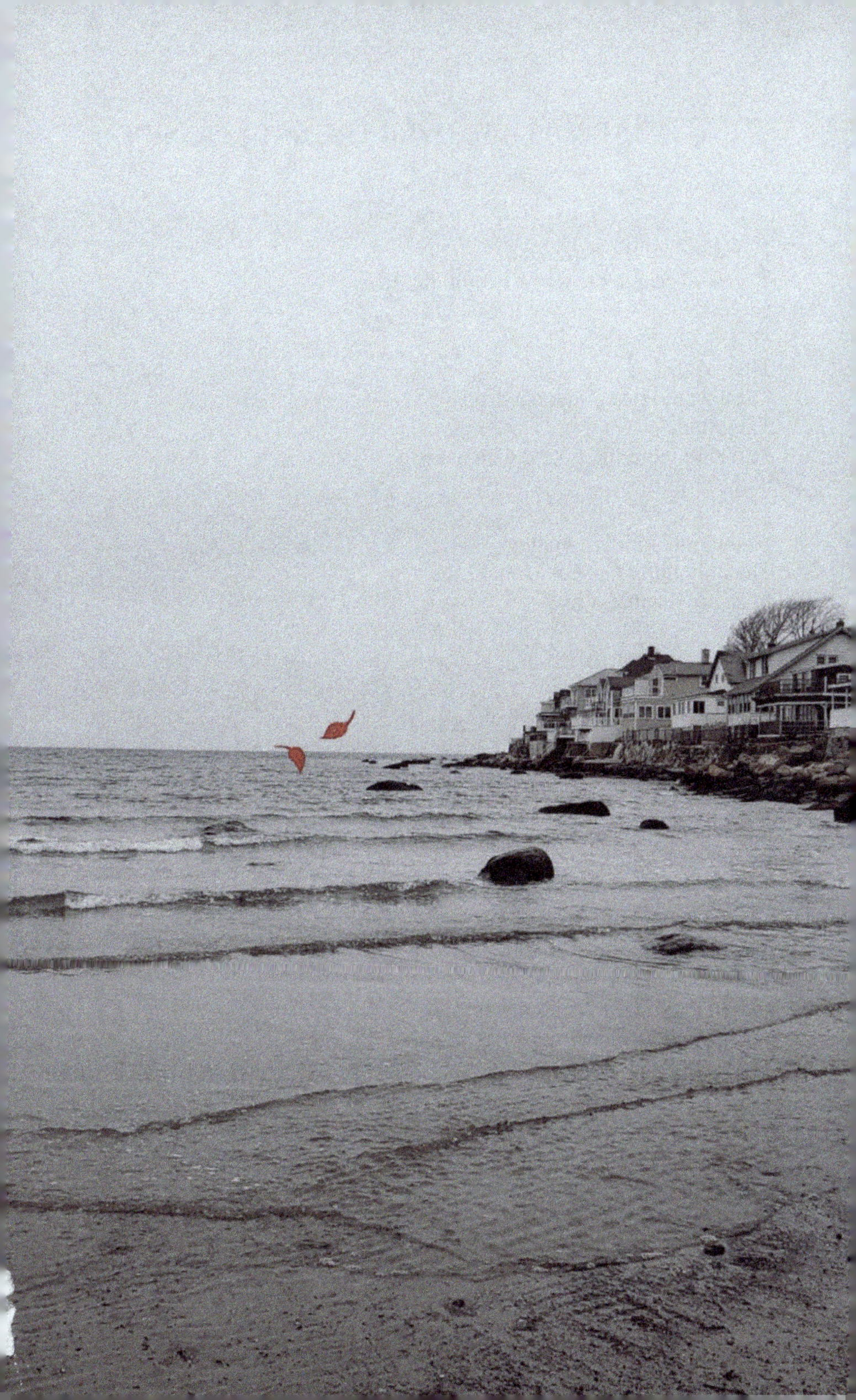

AEROPLANE OVER THE COUNTRYSIDE

I used to fear the aeroplane.
The sky became the terror I could fall from
endlessly.

They said,
"You would just glide, not drop."
They said,
"You are more likely to die on the way
to the airport."

At the time it didn't matter.
The only thing that could shake me
from my relentless fear

was the excitement of
seeing you again.
It was a gleeful, childlike feeling—
it had laid itself
overtop an anxiety that could

no longer consume me.
We ascended into the heavens
& the divine placement of the clouds

mesmerized me.
We grazed the sky smoothly
and all I could think about was you.
When we descended, my heart stopped.
The moments leading up to

seeing you again,
laying my eyes on the
angles of your face,

the seductive curves of your neck—
my heart didn't beat for several hours.
The blood rushed through my body again,
fiery hot, face flushed and burning,
when you finally stood before me.

Again, I was brutally alive,
brutally human.
The sun set at dawn there,

with a night so thick with
sinful temptations,
I could barely keep my hands
to myself.
I wanted to be the one to conquer you,

with my foot firmly pressed on your chest,
feeling your brutally human
heartbeat in my roots—

and to feel your lips on mine
under the stars
in the streets of our old city.
I had dreamt about it for months.
Instead, I squeezed your arms

playfully after you had had a few drinks.
When I ascended again
in the drowning night

on that fateful aeroplane,
I wept silently into the
blackened clouds—
Touchless and Kiss-less.

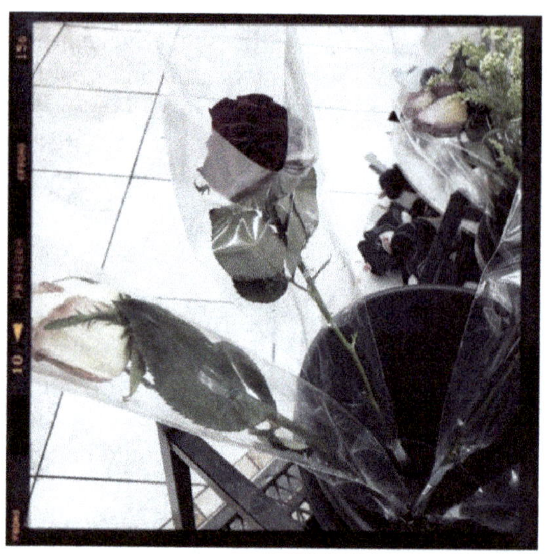

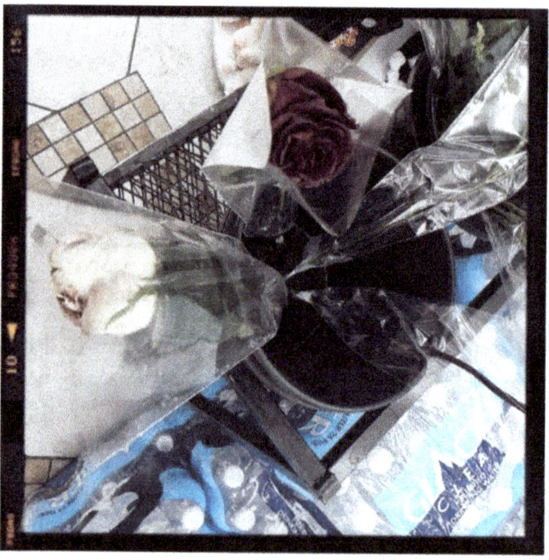

GAS STATION ROSES

You are nervous – it's a constant truth,
and I think I forgot that was your nature.

The way you are – the you I forgot,
gives me the slightest hope ;;
a drop of sweet milk from a
tender but empty breast.

I immediately thought of you
when my tired eyes fixed themselves
on the wilted and darkening red
of the rose bouquets at the gas station—
an odd but beautiful sight,
though I'm not sure what that
says about me or
how I feel about you.

I am nervous, but not like you ;;
you are always rattling within your bones
and I am a low humming—
our frequencies differ,
but I think it's beautiful ::

like finding bouquets of red roses
at the gas station.

27

Sometimes in the morning I think of Jim Morrison,
and when the Sun has peaked at noon,
I think of Jimi Hendrix—
but when I'm sobbing uncontrollably
in my car,
nighttime falling steadily in the distance,
I remember the day Amy Winehouse died—
and sometimes Kurt Cobain watches me
in my sleep and I remember
that I'm 27 now.

I've never been so terrified of my age,
thinking I wasted all my time
changing my mind and being
frustratingly inconsistent.

If seventeen year-old me could see me now,
I think she would be disappointed
that I never became a singer,
only belting solemnly in my lonely car
stranded somewhere I never imagined.

But if Lana could revel in her debut at 27,
then what's stopping me from becoming
a poet at the same age?
Seeing as how I never developed any
musical talent.

After all, words are just words—
it's all the same,
and I'm finally building a sturdy brick house
where I stand today.

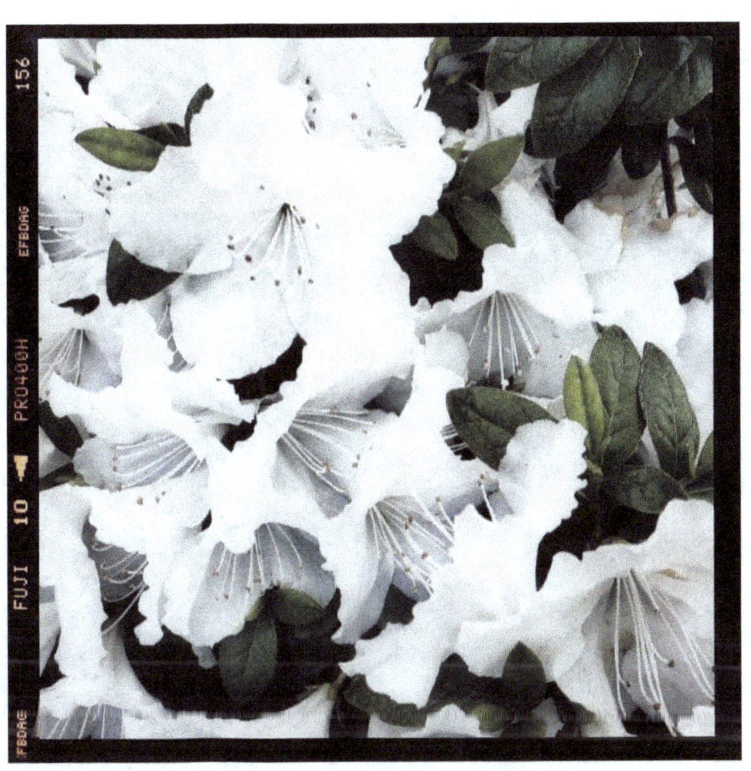

FUJI 10 PRO400H EFBDAG 156
FBDAG

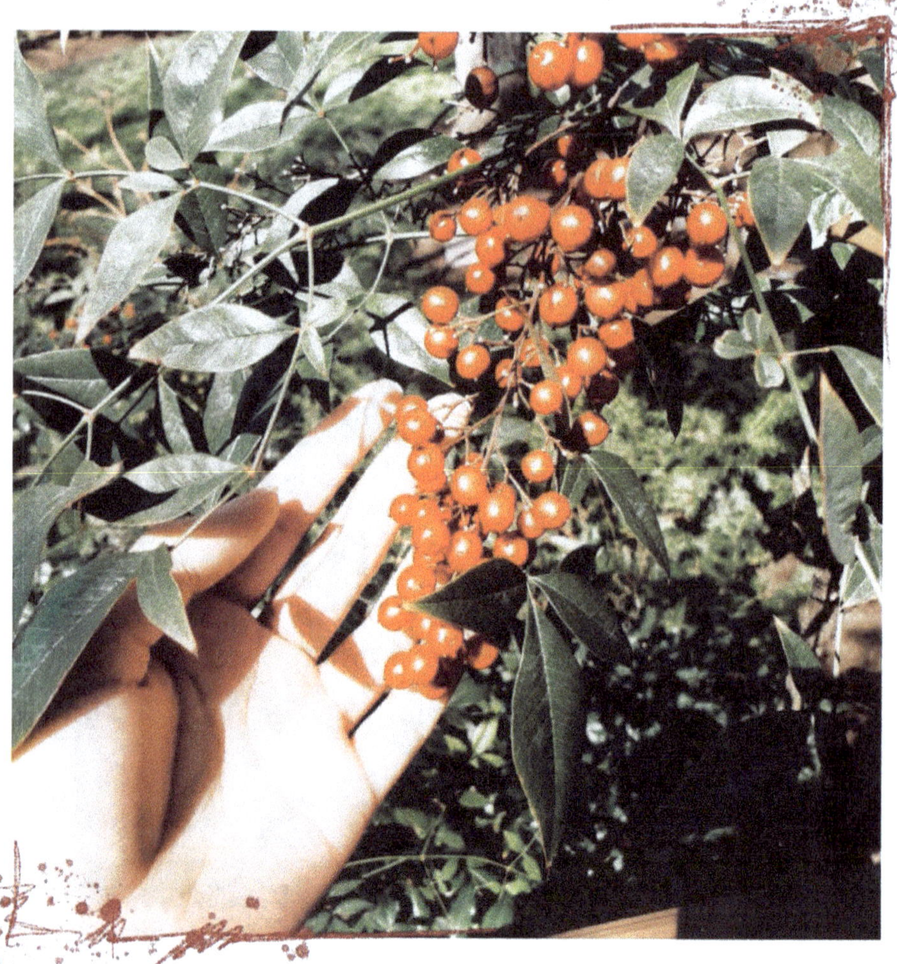

THE LOVE WITCH

I pulled a spell from the foggy ether—
with decorated red candle sticks
and thick rose petals to match ;;
pink salt and a basin
for intentions set ablaze.

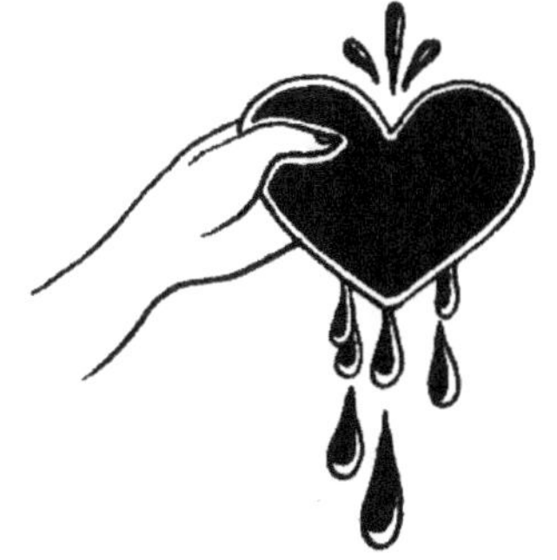

Behind closed bedroom doors,
morals and ethics cease to exist
as I know what I want
& what I want is you.

It's cliché, I know,
but my herbs in jars and
gleaming pink and orange crystals
are all that keep me hopeful.

Lilith blessed me with
a sharp tongue to keep me blunt
and seductive while
Aphrodite gifted me numerous
crystalized sea shells and
a feather-light laugh—
to be a daughter with
two celestial mothers who
watch me and
who I fall in love with,
as The Wheel of Fortune
is always turning.

And with enough sugar and
loving divine timing,
I know you will be mine someday,
whenever & wherever that may be.

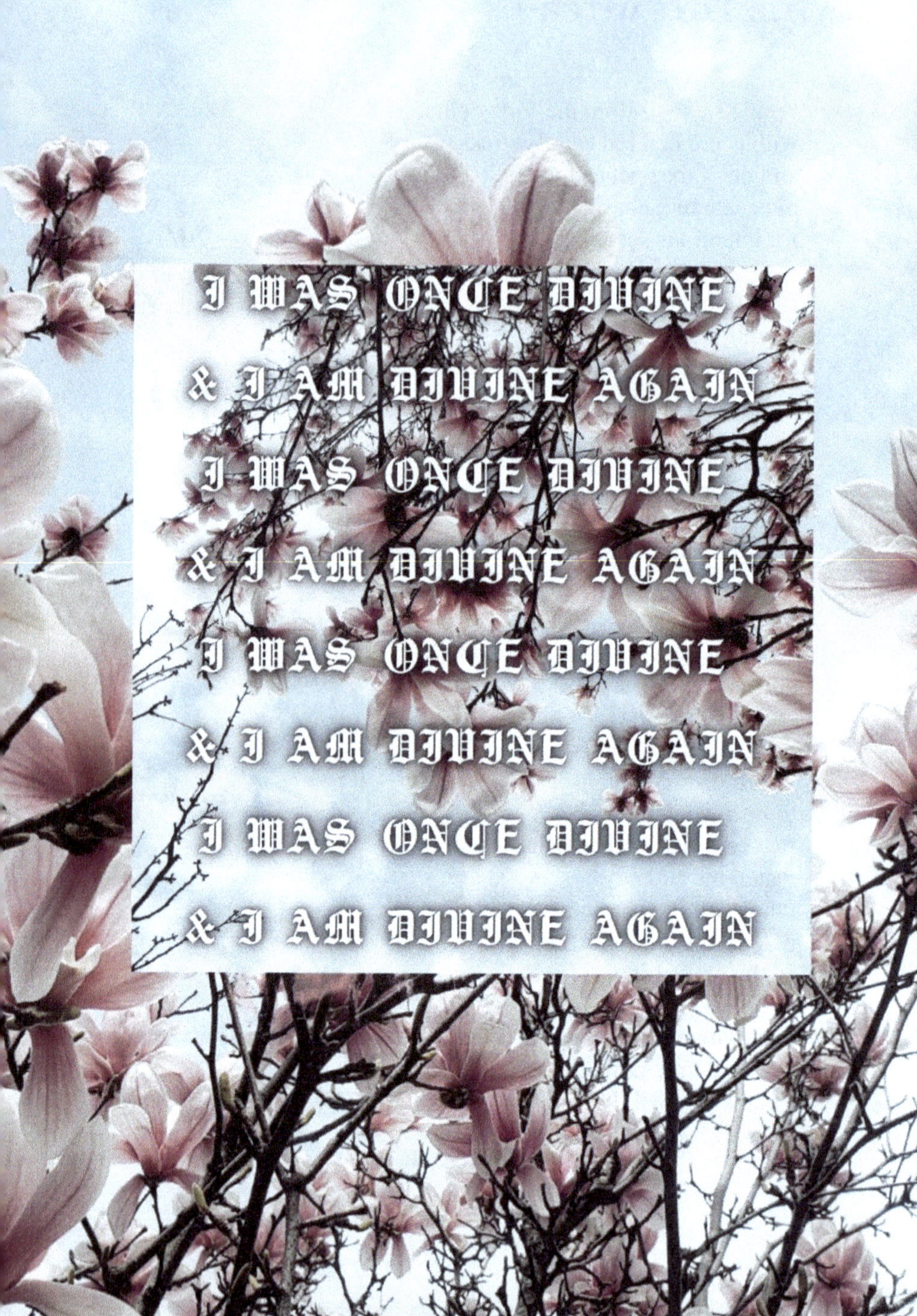
I WAS ONCE DIVINE
& I AM DIVINE AGAIN
I WAS ONCE DIVINE
& I AM DIVINE AGAIN
I WAS ONCE DIVINE
& I AM DIVINE AGAIN
I WAS ONCE DIVINE
& I AM DIVINE AGAIN

GODHOOD IS MY HEART

Godhood is a title I earned through my human suffering.

A rose opens up into the world for the Sun & air to wilt its delicate divinity.
Girlhood was my birthright and
Godhood is my fateful ascension.

As vast as the ocean and as endless as the cosmos that
Watches us cry and ache—
Watches us laugh and sing.

I would twist and braid those roses into my rolling curls if I never
Get the chance to give them to you.

I learned to love myself through the constellations
embedded in my skin
And the splitting ends of my hair ;;

With hummingbirds buzzing about,
Admiring the duality of my divinity—

Through gentle human passion and the cosmic atlas of the galaxy
In my red and wet eyes.

Many reflections of my past guide me through the delicate enigma of my future.
If I was painted on a canvas,
Those constellations would glisten beautifully in the golden hour of dusk.

Godhood is a title I earned
Through my overflowing heart,
Swollen with aching humanity
And passionate yearning
For someone who is just beyond my reach.

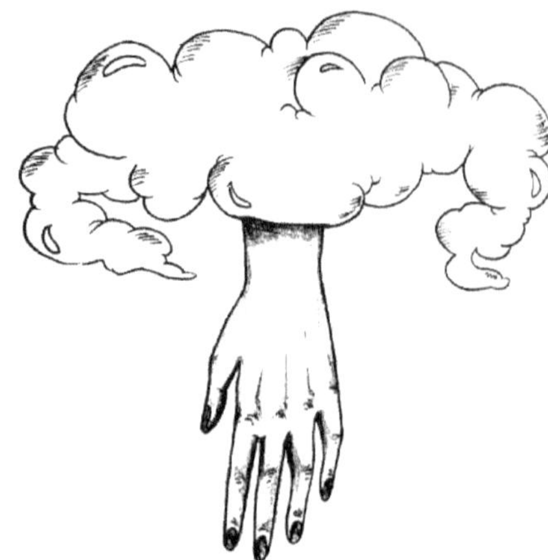

EVANESCENT AS SMOKE FROM PARTED LIPS

I was just another shrink appointment
when I was always meant to be
The cigarette smoke that left my lips—

The wisps born from the cherried wick
of a freshly blown-out candle—
Thin and disappearing ;

Never meant to stay,
Never meant to linger.

But somehow I was encased inside four stone walls that felt like
A sweet and loving embrace,
but I could never see over them,
And I rotted in permanent shade with no hope of the Sun.

I was just another "girl who got away"
One, two, maybe three times ;

They say :
"Leaving you was my biggest regret,"
"I'm sorry I treated you like shit when we were together,"

As if I only deserved better when, and only when,
I was no longer theirs'.
As if my gore-ridden fits of sobbing were never
justified when I broke
Over and over again.

I was just another headache Tylenol couldn't fix
When I was never meant to stay in the same place.

My bones and my skin keep me solid when I was always meant to
fade away
And wander as I please.

Release me from these walls, the grip I'm trapped in,
Because I ache and quiver for a different tender and
loving embrace.
I can move states all I want,
But I will always carry an aspect of the truth I am desperate to
leave behind.

Love me in a way that makes me feel light as air—
You would be the first who didn't force me to be solid.

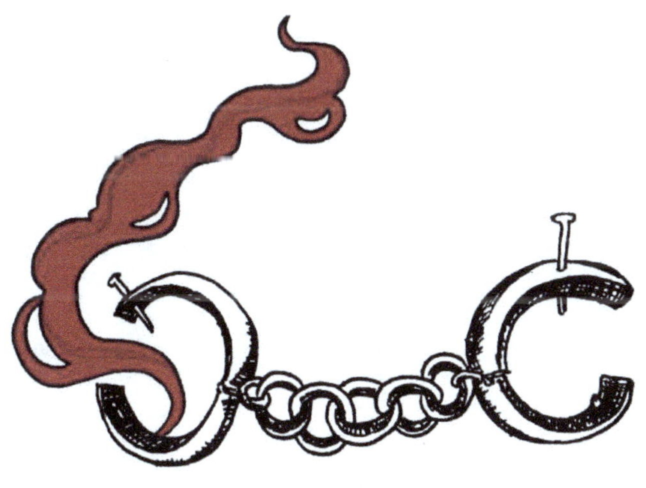

CRUMBS

It's the smallest things sometimes ::
touching my earring, unprompted,
to get a better look at it ;
grazing my hands with your fingertips
when I say how cold they are ;
lightly chuckling at the jokes I make
under my breath
when no one else hears them ;
showing off to me because you know
that I will boost your confidence
with my enthusiasm
no matter what.

It's that we have similar preferences,
grew up alone the same way,
how we are both too creative
to do simple math,
and we are both captivated by
Black & Gold.

But at the end of the day,
when I'm alone in my bed,
I have to tell myself that
what is making my heart flutter
uncontrollably
is fucking crumbs.

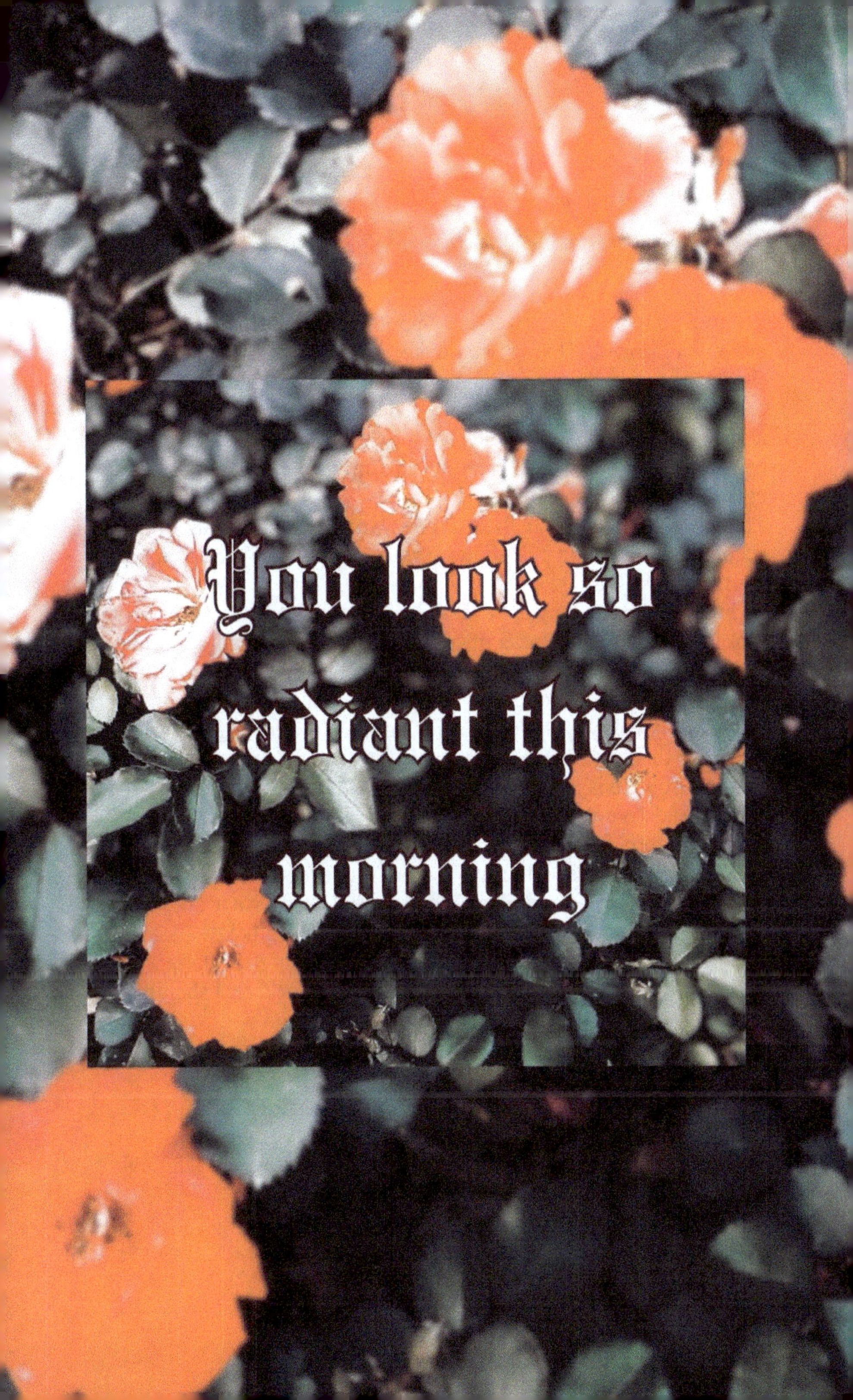
You look so
radiant this
morning

RAISON D'ÊTRE

To give you so much power and importance over me and say you are my reason for living would be the grandest overstatement. Because my power lies within me, ~~you are not on a pedestal~~. ~~If you are my Tower, then how could you also be my Star?~~ And maybe you are just the vessel that propelled me forward from a life of the purely mundane into something freer, where my words might actually make a difference.

To claim you as my *raison d'être* would diminish all of my accomplishments and pull all those who actually love me down into Hell.

So here I am, bringing you down to eye level, so now you may really look at me – the puffiness of my eyes, the bumps and scars that adorn my face. May you be completely consumed by the vortex within my honey eyes and may you see yourself fully through them. Because, in reality, you've given me nothing, ~~no fucking reason~~ for me to be this heart-shattered over you, to live in such agony over you. All you are is just a sweet and pretty boy – ~~and god, you are so pretty~~. And I've been relearning my own divinity and worshiping my own infernal existence.

You brought softness into my life when I needed debauchery. You made my heart beat and bleed when I didn't even want one. You made me feel human when I was meant to feel Godlike. ~~If I am the love witch, you are simply my next victim, not the God I pray to.~~

I should be your reason for existing, your *raison d'être*. I should be haunting your dreams, ~~making you sweat, twisting and stirring in your bed, licking your lips and salivating – absolutely ravenous for one small taste of my silk-wrapped skin. Your heart should be an open and gushing wound you carry around, barely containing the spills of gold-laced blood, leaving trails with every step you take.~~

You are not my burden to bear. You are not the stake I carry through my heart. How enticing am I to you, if I even exist?

I believed your mind was beautiful; a landscape I desperately wanted to lose myself in. ~~But I repeatedly found there was no space for myself there~~. How on earth could you be my *raison d'être* if you keep your heart locked inside a steel cage? I can gaze at it, but never could I graze it, hold it gently like a sparrow in my bloody hands.
~~If this is a bible for you, then let my newfound contemptuous disdain of my feelings for you be the scripture others recite ignorantly. Because there is no fucking way I could truly allow myself to fall apart over a man.~~

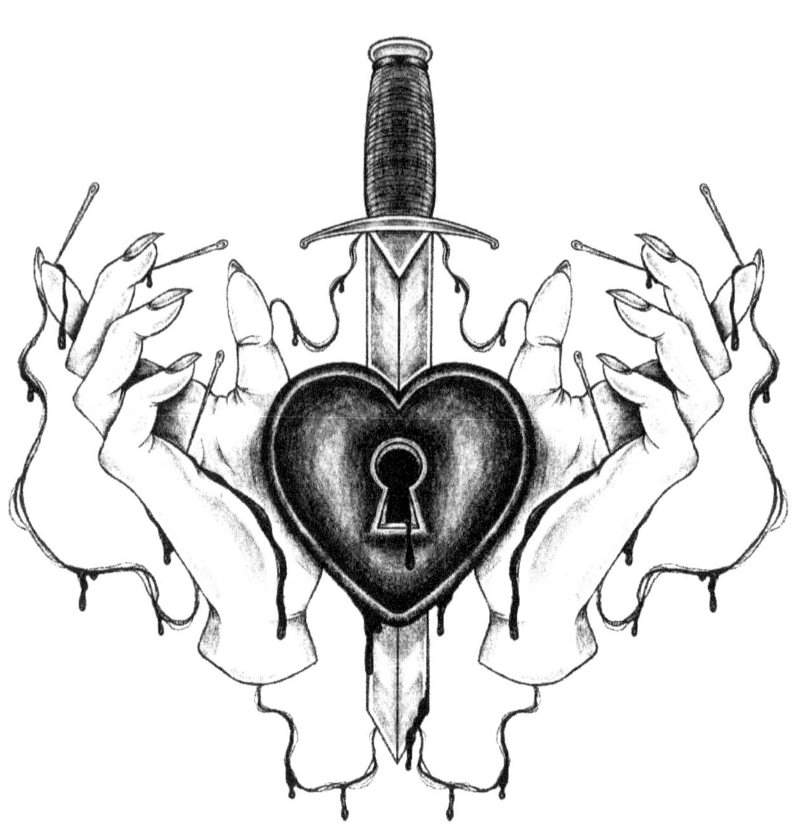

it's all I have.

ETERNITY IS A ROTTING SUMMER

it's all I have.

STAR GIRL MANIFESTO

I draw the blinds open every morning because the natural light cleanses and feeds my soul.

I always make my coffee with ground cinnamon to enhance my intentions and manifestations.

I am the star whose crystalized fragments shine brightest in the moonless-dark.

I am everything and nothing and all the quiet and undisturbed places in between.

I spend my afternoons dancing skyclad with my divine mothers around a crimson fire.

I am the one that haunts the Devil's dreams and
who he fears in his waking hours.

I am the forest nymph who coughs up leaves and
whose nose runs with tree sap.

I will dance in my finest dress on your grave if
you dare go before me.

don't go

I will ask my star-sisters for your dreams
when you disappear - it's all I have.

I clutch my locket to my breast so my beating
heart will breathe life into it.

When I am lost, I never want to be found - I
will find you underneath the vibrant night sky
when I want a kiss goodnight.

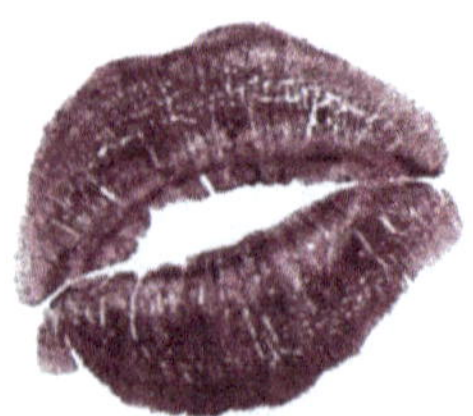

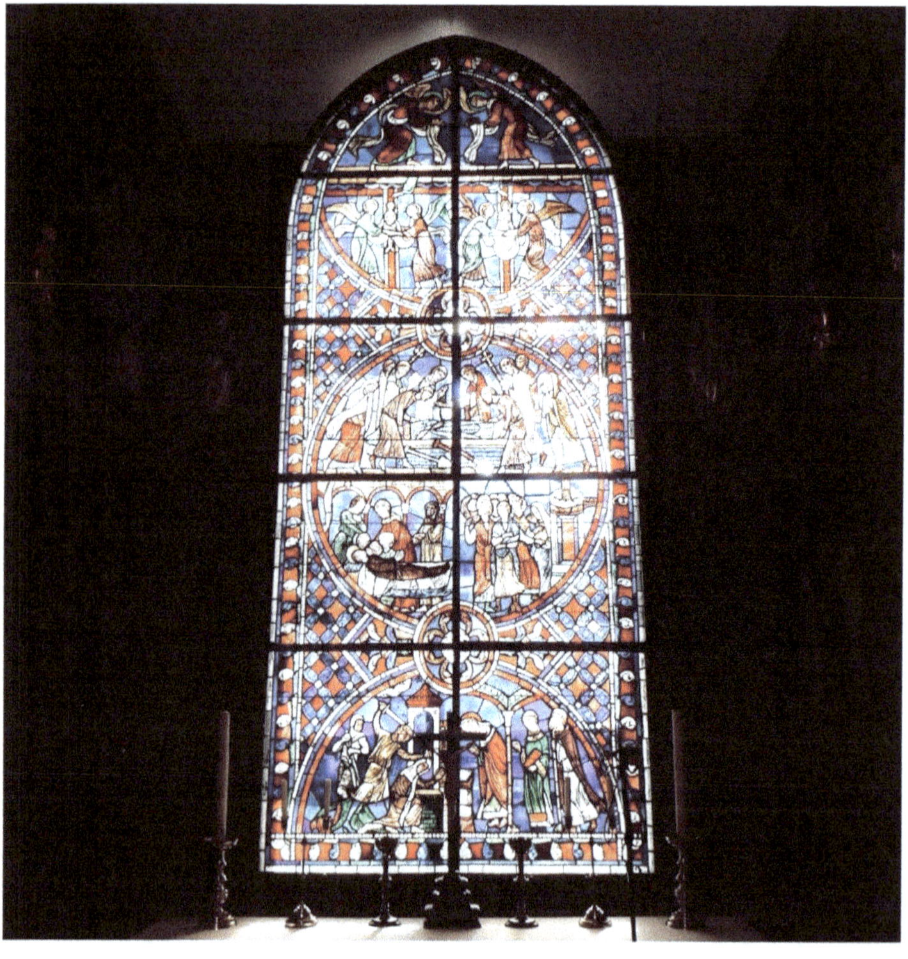

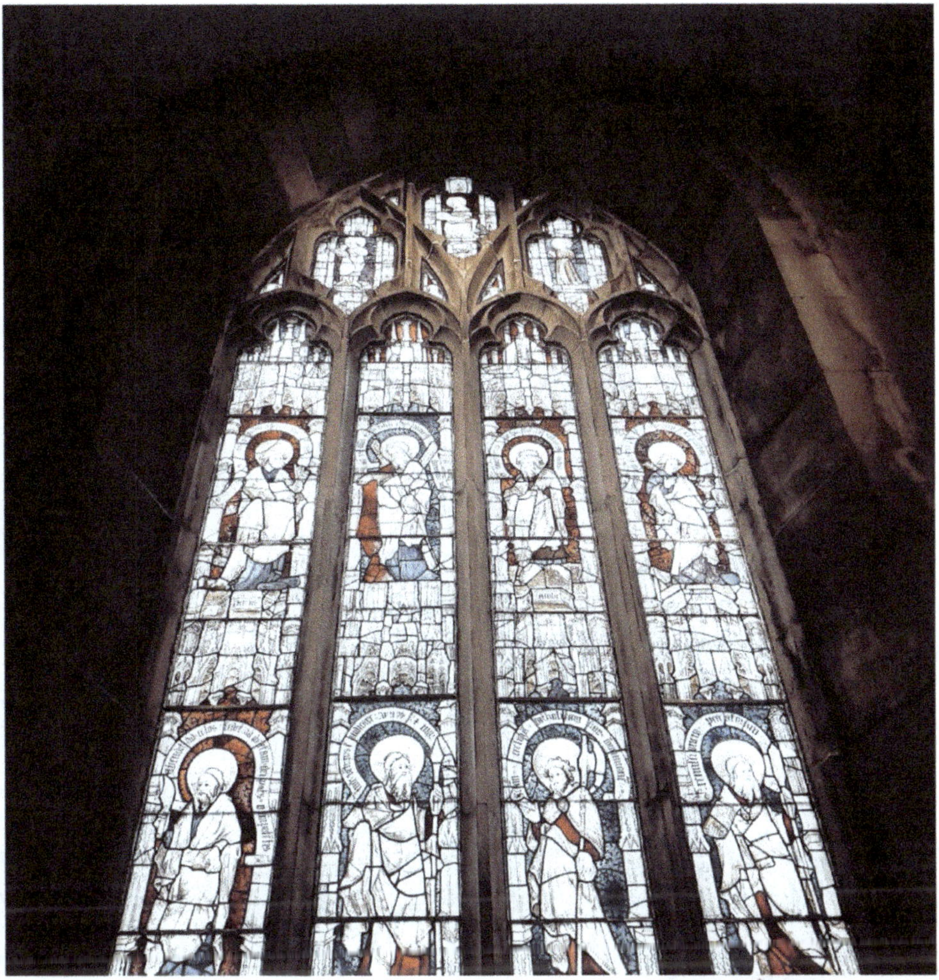

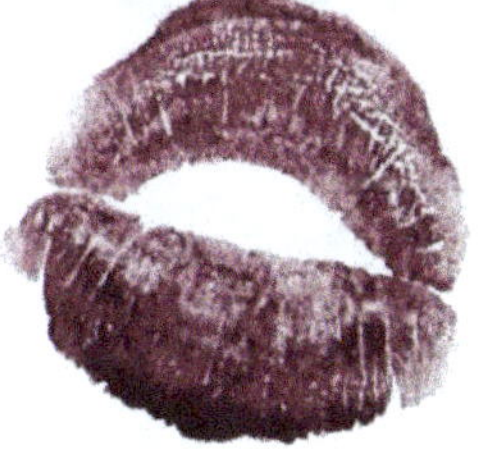

OUTSTRETCHED INTO THE ETHER

I was yours all along,
silly boy,
You just didn't know it.

You were stuck in your

Sunny Wonderland Dream,
Unaware that I was always there.

And of course I forgive you,
You know I do—

I just had to detach myself
From the idea that you

Were being malicious.
I slept on the couch because

I spoke my truth,
And that's when I stopped existing,

Stopped breathing the same air,
Stopped gazing at the same stars.

I forgive you, of course,
You know I do.

The Sun became harsher
As the days grew shorter—

And I will always miss you
Even if we never cross paths again—

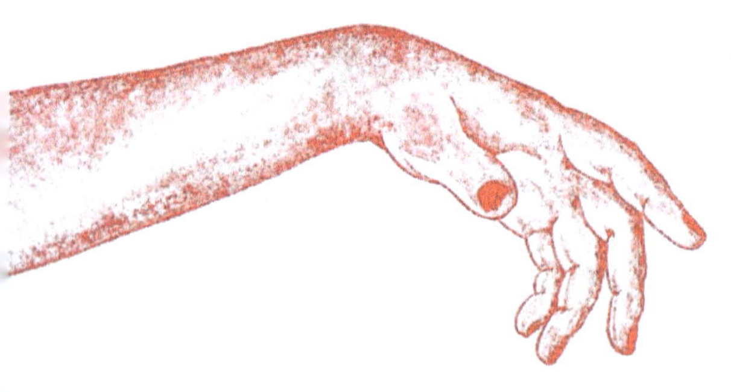

You are undeniably the
Special and ethereal love

That I will always remember,
Always hold onto,

Even if you come back
to my realm
And love me the way I
always

Dreamt of.
My body was never a temple
because

I will always be brutally
human,
Brutally aching for you.

And as the days grow longer,

I hope the love will grow
with them,

But I will forgive you
if it doesn't.
There will always be a flame
within me

For you – my heart
outstretched
Into the ether for you,

Even if it doesn't meet
anything
On the other side.

I will always be yours,
silly boy,
Even if you never know it.

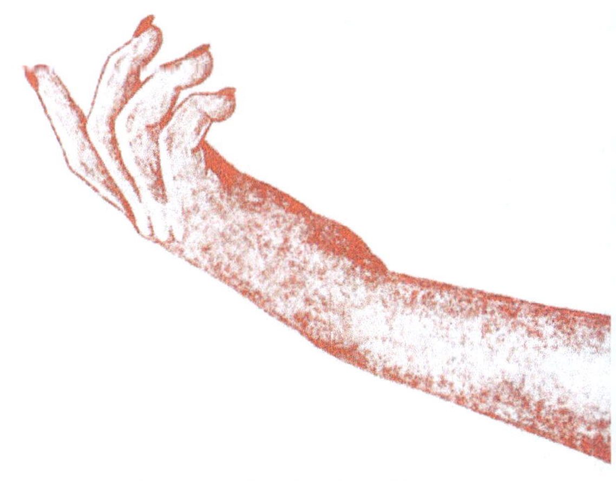

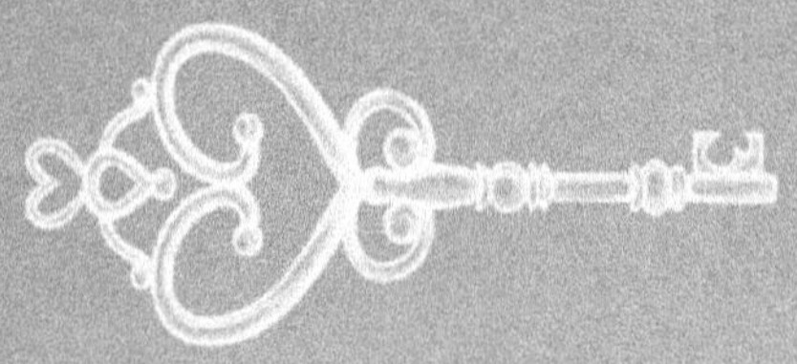

I found a home in your gentle
embrace
and mistook it for our old
dusty city

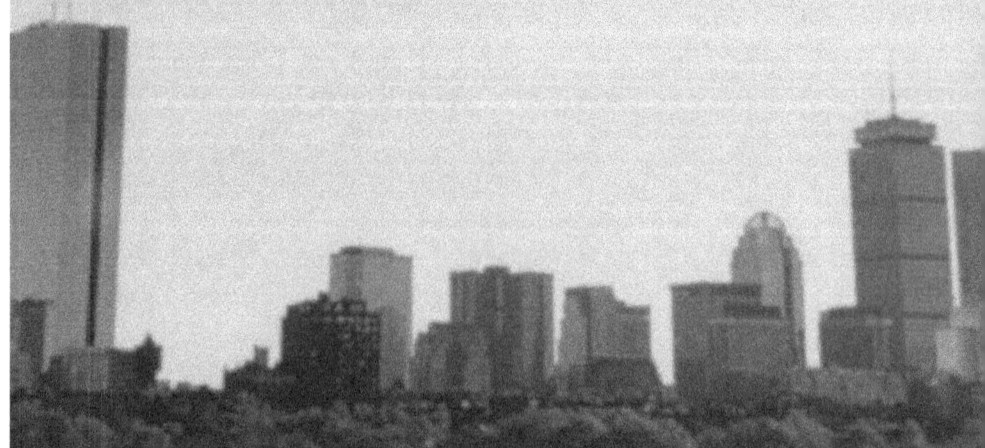

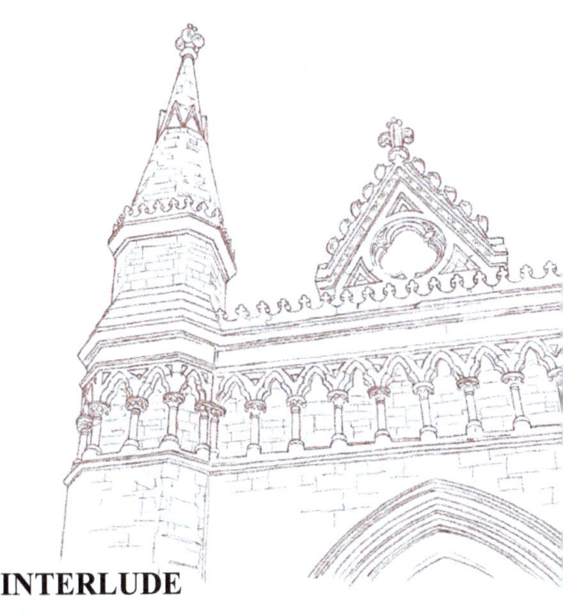

INTERLUDE

The years had passed in a daze, and we barely spoke. What was once a beautiful and lavish dream became an all-consuming nightmare. A terror full of panic and profound sadness that had enveloped my daily life in the way a snake unhinges its jaw to consume its prey whole. In every instance, I thought of you. And the way in which I thought of you was harmful and intoxicating, a feeling I easily fell victim to, became hopelessly addicted to. It was such a vile and deplorable way of life. I constantly thought of what fragrances and lipsticks to buy, how to color and style my hair, even how to seduce you with my eyes and lips. In a twisted way, I lost my own human authenticity while somehow growing infernally divine. I became insanely jealous of every woman that could cross your path, never thinking that maybe you wouldn't be interested in the idea of pursuit altogether. (Though, it was possible that I could be the exception.) And it was all the small teases of hope I clung onto, the ones I fed myself. I had to remain positive and aligned, and that became my superstition – as if you could read my thoughts across state lines. All that I was doing, and of course I was completely aware, was constantly deluding myself. I had created a dream I could travel to whenever I closed my eyes, and that glistening place was in your arms. And after all this time, I think all I really did was create a version of you that was perfect – a version of you that doesn't actually exist, (though, I hope with all my heart, that it does.)

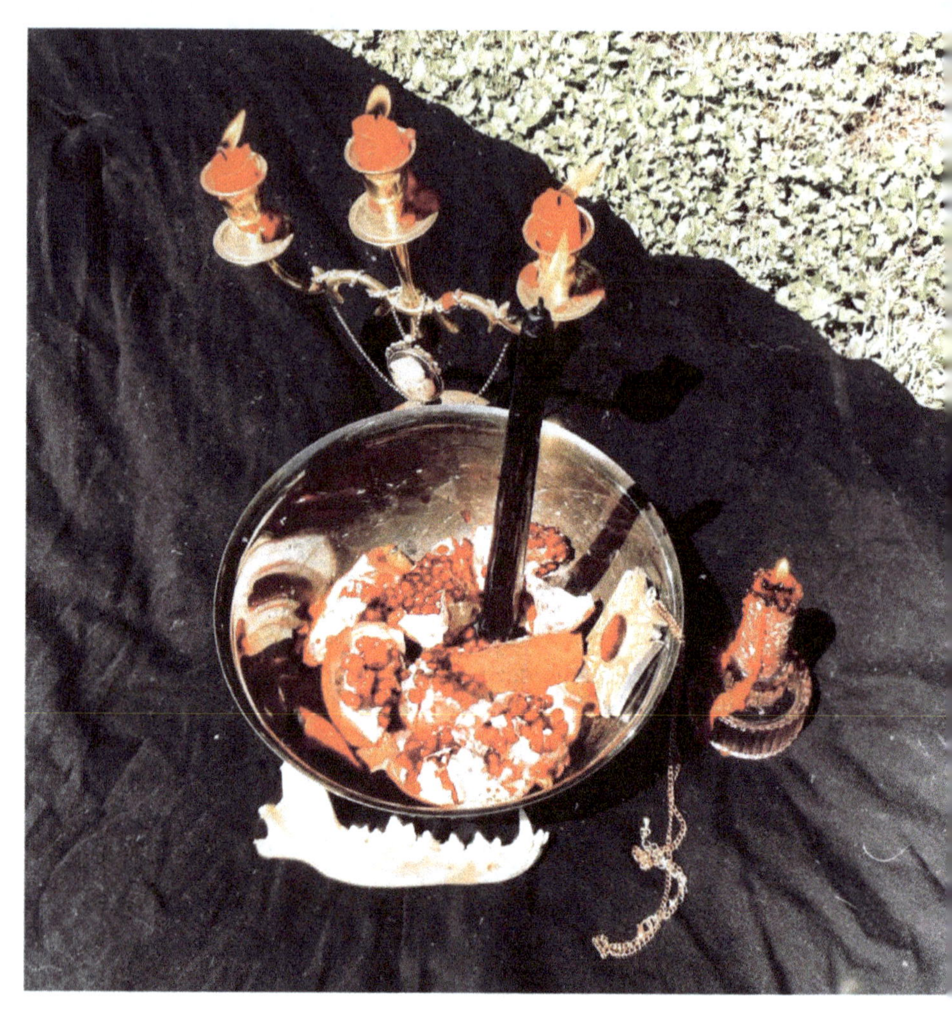

" I SAW THE FACE OF GOD
AND IT WAS HER BEAUTIFUL FACE
AND SHE WAS SO RADIANT ...

AND I WAS SO TERRIFIED BUT FULLY CONSUMED BY PLEASURE."

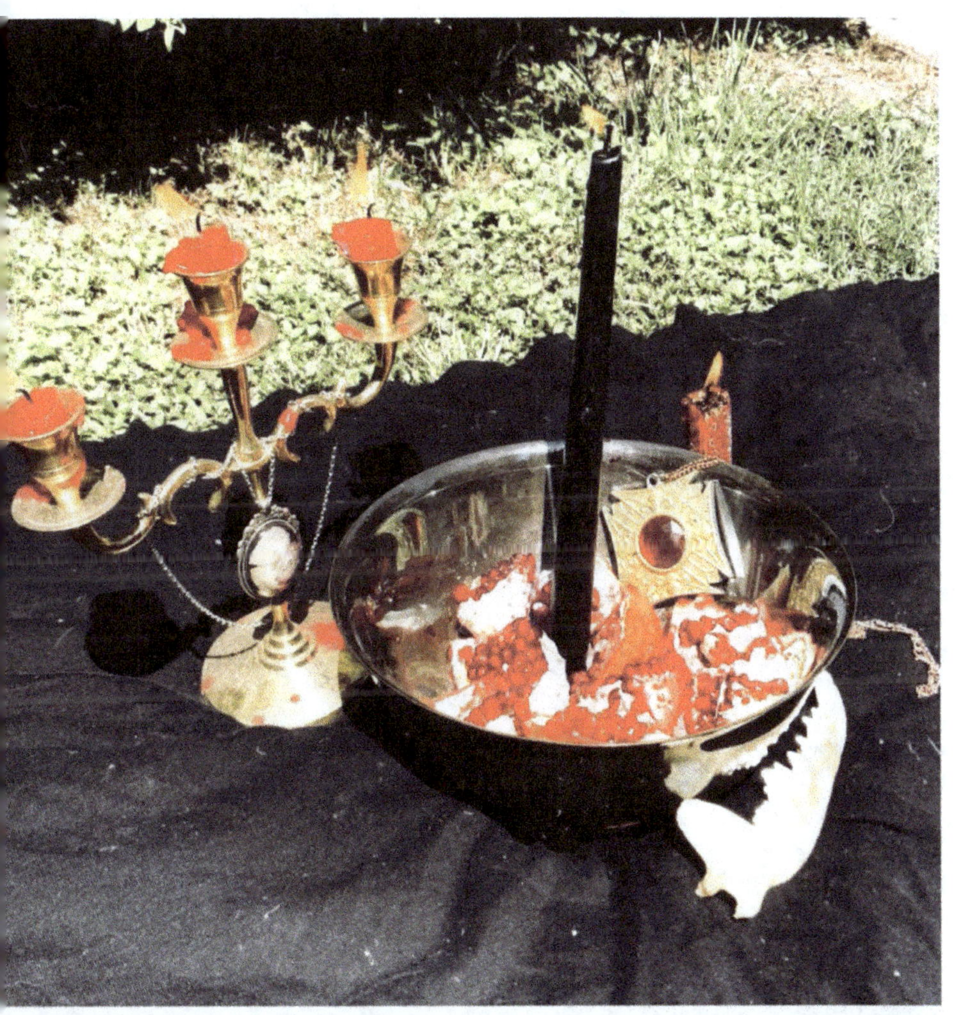

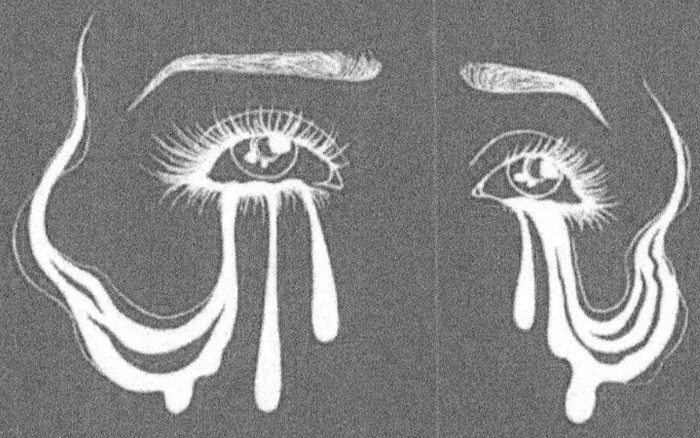

TURN ME INTO A FLOWER

- iv -

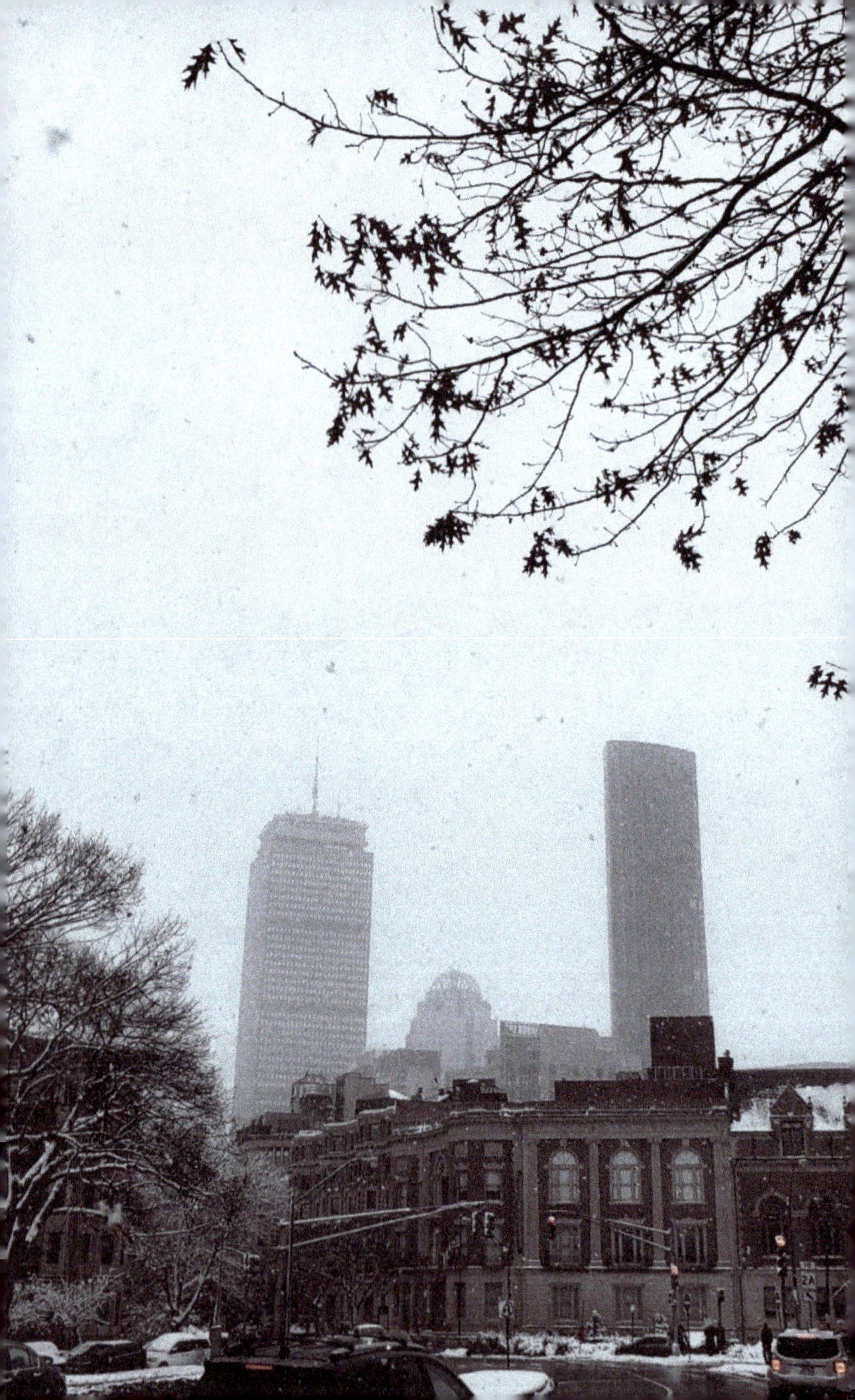
2A

AFTER WE PARTED WAYS

Oh, how I wish you would stop taunting me through the ether.
I know that is where I primarily exist,
But I crave your physical touch.

I reached my shaking hand out to meet yours,
but was met with the coldness of
Nothingness.

You could take the next flight out to see me,
Or I to you,
But my messages are usually left unread.

And I somehow blame myself
for having the kind of energy that must be pushing you away;
Though I'm not known for my nonchalance.

Oh, how I wish you would stop taunting me through the ether
and just reach your hand out to meet mine.

LUNAR DESTRUCTION

The *Secret* came out
Under the light of the Full Moon.

I released you from the locket around my neck,
With feverish wailing,
Crying and shedding—
You came out free into my world.

I speak your name without hesitation.
I speak your name without shame or guilt.
I speak your name because I love how it feels
rolling off my tongue.
I speak your name because I adore how it tastes.

After so long of keeping you stored away
As my deepest desire, my ultimate *Secret*
Inside the heart-shaped locket around my neck,
I can finally breathe your name into my world
And feel a small sense of bliss.

I've lit a hundred candles with the energy of your name,
Lighting up my nights with the Dark Moon Goddess,
& praying that my sister stars take my whispers to your ears.

I shed the regrets of my past—
I feel you in my dreams,
Touching my arms,
My neck,
Holding my face in your hands
Through the ether.

When I dream of you,
I hope you dream of me too.

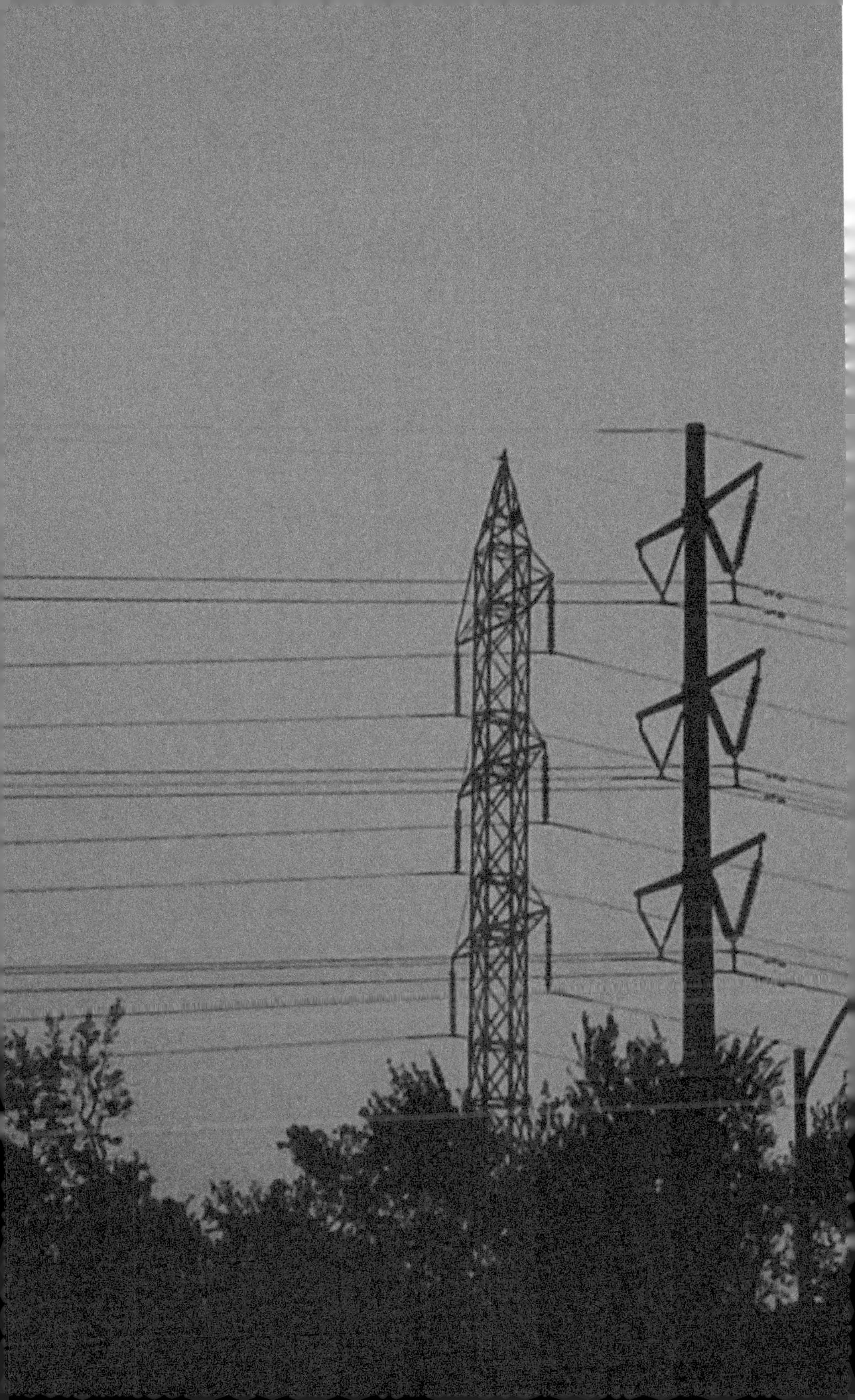

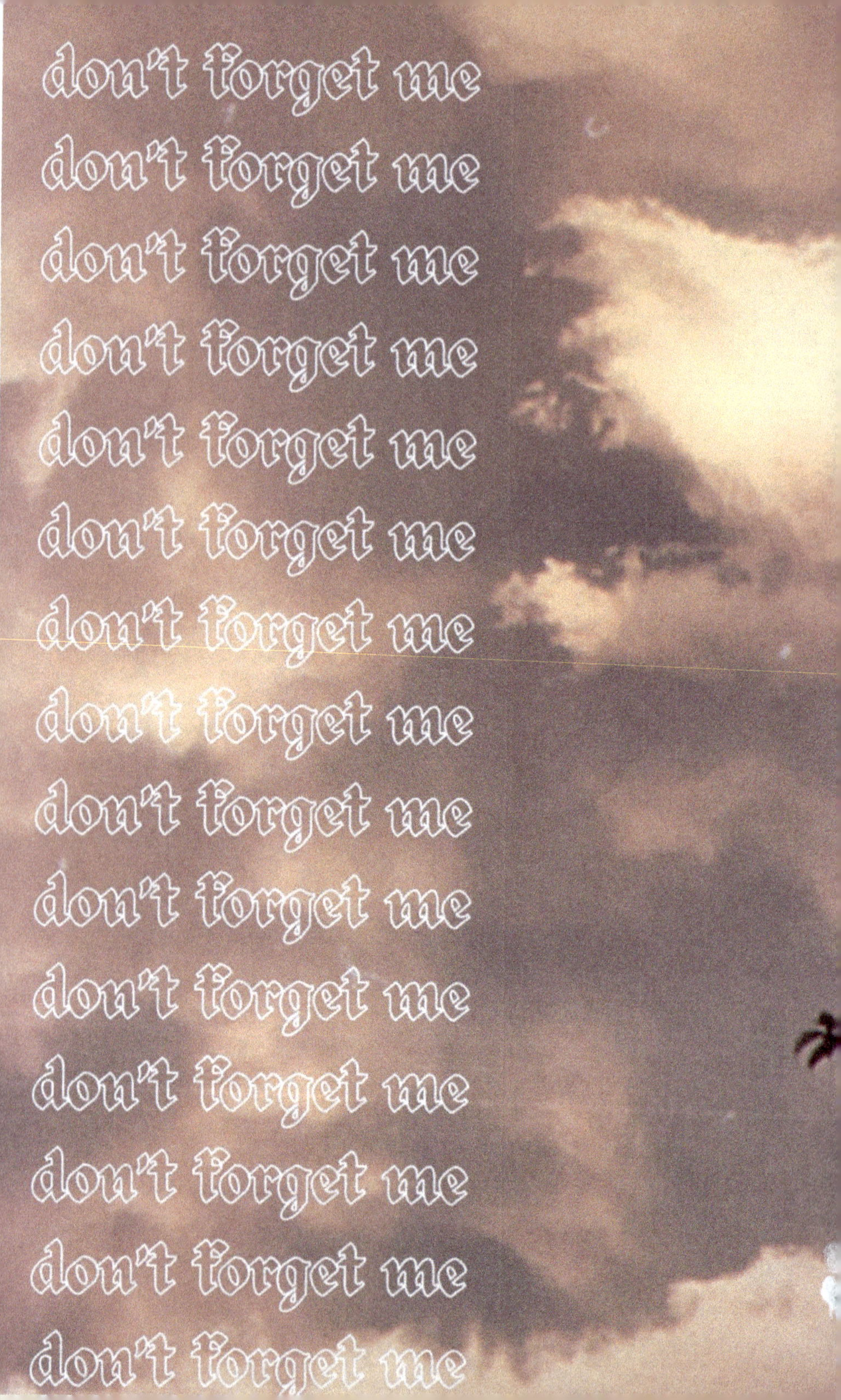

don't forget me
don't forget me
don't forget me
don't forget me
don't forget me
don't forget me
don't forget me
don't forget me
don't forget me
don't forget me
don't forget me
don't forget me
don't forget me
don't forget me
don't forget me

DON'T FORGET ME NOW THAT WE'RE APART

I notice you
and the way you move,
the way you talk,
the way you are.

i. How you hold yourself,
slightly curled up,
as if you are your only safe
space—
to exist as your authentic
self.

ii. How you intensely rub
your hands together
when you're nervous,
& the way you chuckle shyly
rather
than let yourself laugh fully.

iii. How you cannot make
eye contact
when you're talking,
as if the sky has kinder eyes
for you to gaze into.

iv. How it takes hours for
you to reply
to messages
or read them just to never
respond.
They all say ::

"I haven't heard from him in
months."

v. And how you finally shine
your brightest
after several drinks.

I don't think you mean to.
I think you can't help it.
And I know because of

vi. how you
can start a conversation with
great ease,
as if your mind is always
buzzing with ideas.

vii. How you show genuine
interest
in the words you hear.

You wanted to know more
about me
and you understood me
when I said I'm
uncomfortable
having a body.

I could spend an eternity
talking to you
the way we did that night—

and you said I'm an artist no
matter what.

I want to learn everything
about you
and hear you talk endlessly
about your life;
to finally understand the true
complexities
of your mind.

I want to see the
layers of you
that you don't show to
anyone else,
even when you're drunk.

I know you're always
thinking—
your mind racing and
unsteady.

I want to hear it all,
every last thought,
and watch your face light up
when you talk.

If we were always in the
same room,
I think it would be easy—
but you are so far away,
I know I don't exist
anymore.

Though before, I know I did
just a little bit.
You used to watch me
silently
through your phone,
read all the nonsense
I would post,
and give me occasional
hearts.

And oh, how those hearts
tasted so sweet,
I always craved more,
though that was all you had
to give.

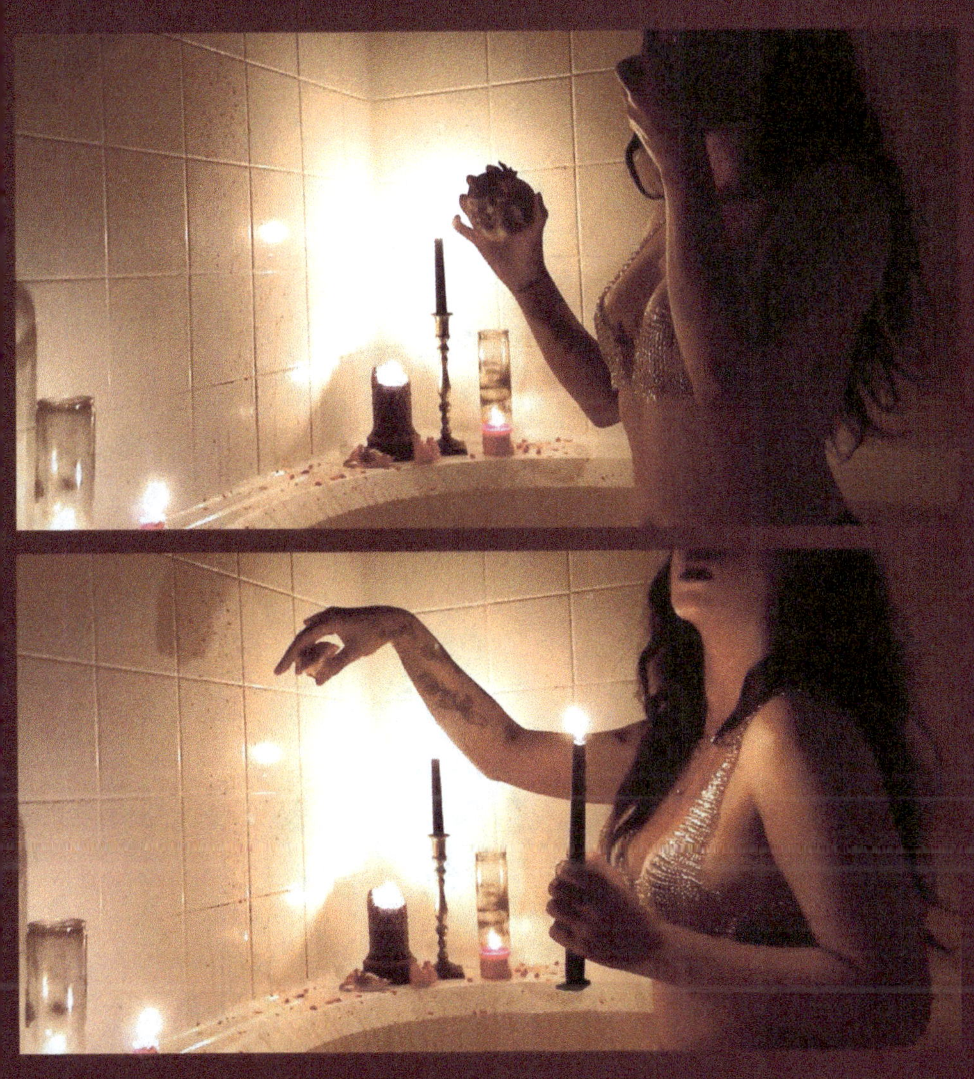

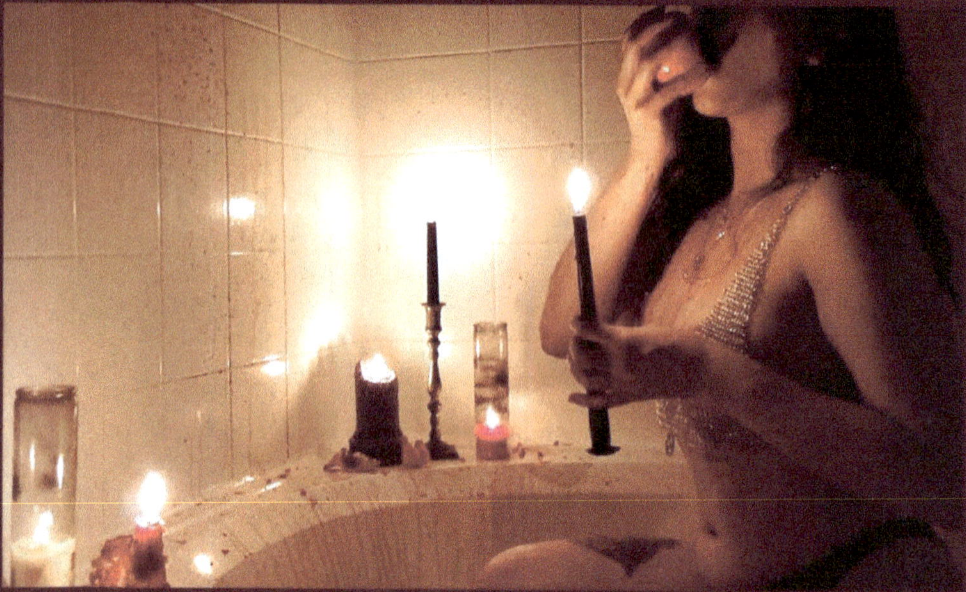

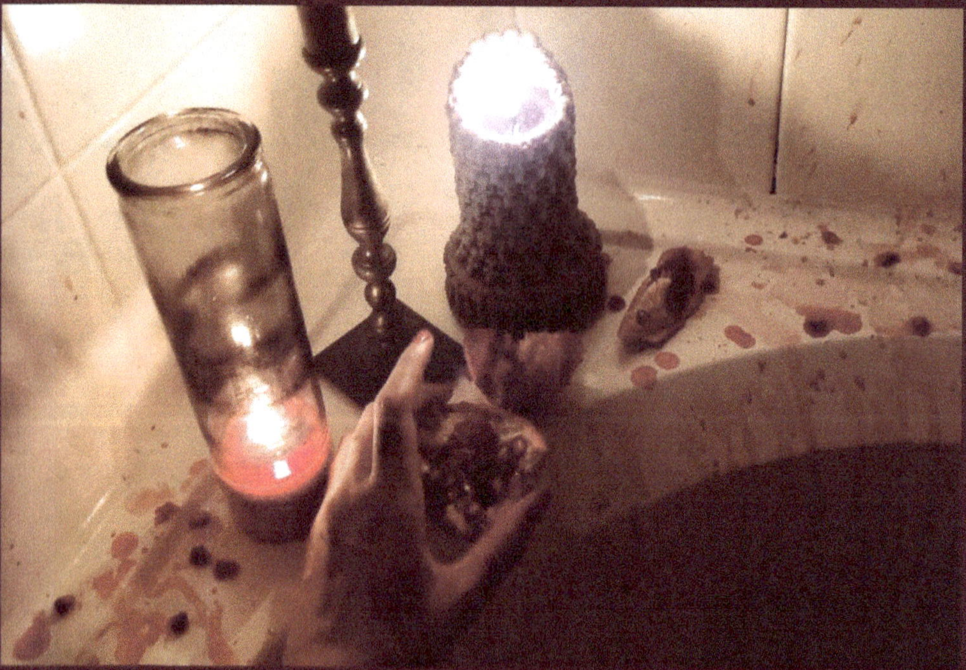

YOU.

There's a million and one
things I could have written about.
A million and one
ideas in my head—
and all I can get myself to write about
is *you.*

And I hate myself so much because
I am as vast as the ocean,
as endless as the cosmos above—
I have so much more inside of me,
but all I can create,
all I can write about
is *you.*

I painted so much because of *you*—
of lockets and heartstrings and tears ;;
because I didn't have any words
at the time.
So much paint & paper,
so many brushes I used up because
of *you.*

In a way, I should thank *you*
for being my muse,

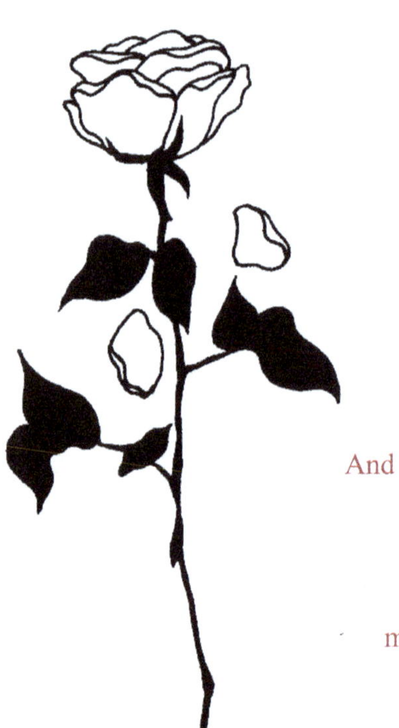

for forcing me to display my yearning
on a pedestal
for the whole world to see.

But I know that without *you*
I am still shining & infinite—
my mind swarming with
a million and one
crystallized thought forms
from the stars that watch me,
sing to me,
and mourn with me.

And in the overwhelming crowded vastness
of my shattered mind,
within a million and one
fragmented ideas,
you remain the only constant,
my only true and divine sense of clarity.

Though, I know these words
will hurt some,
confuse some,
and even bore some—
these words are not for them.
They will always be *yours*.

DISCARDED WHORE PLEASE IGNORE

THE CURSE OF A FREE WOMAN

Maybe you stopped looking at me
because you found out that I'm a
Free Woman.

I'd like to think it's because,
now that I'm a
Free Woman,
I'm suddenly intimidating,
and my eyes now give you feelings
you'd rather hide from.

I'd like to imagine that now
I haunt your dreams
and you wake up in a panicked sweat
filled to the brim with lust
[*The Devil*],
and maybe even envy
of all those who have touched me before.

And maybe, I hope,
that you fantasize about me
unintentionally—
and with every passing moment,
your heart beats harder & faster.

But maybe I'm just hopeful,
for I do not truly know
how you feel,
what you think,
or what you're doing
now that you know that I'm a
Free Woman.

INSIDE V. OUTSIDE

I don't want to be out there in the *Great Unknown* that is reality.

I have found a home inside myself where I can bask in my delusional fantasies, and the vibrancy of my inner world.
I would rather be in here than out there.

Because out there, life is completely loveless and has been for so long I don't remember anything different.
Out there, you don't text, you don't call, you don't hop on the next flight to kiss me passionately on the buzzing streets.
Out there, there are no colors, just glimpses of red and blue that taunt me.
Out there, my aching body is touchless, no loving embraces, and no matter how hard I try to magnetize through the ether, there are no kisses from your lips.

At least on the inside there is a beautiful and never-ending story—where you are in love and obsessed with me and I am the one with the cool composure, though still brimming with passion.
On the inside, everything is magnificent and divine because I am my own God, and you caress me with such loving tenderness, my common tears could never convey my true feelings.
The inside is so decadent and filled with such fervent debauchery, but only with you grasping my hand like you will never let go.
Inside, you cherish me in the mornings, and worship me at night, as if mere visions of me grant you great lustful unease.

Out there, you act carelessly and nonchalantly, as if you didn't think muting me wouldn't shatter my heart and send me into a spiral.

On the inside, you kiss me and hold me so tenderly.

On the outside, I'm constantly asking myself "what did I do", "what did I do wrong", "what didn't I do that I should have".

And it's times like these where I think I deserve the blood clots and the gushing – as if my own womb is shredding itself apart along with my own heart.

"Don't minimize yourself," they say,
Though I'm worried I'm too big, too grand, too loud, too blunt.
On the inside, I am perfect how I am, and you love me for it regardless.
It's better inside.

It's better inside

MAYBE I'M NOT REAL

My mentality both strengthened and weakened me, like how a rose's petals are so delicate and soft while its thorns a violent piercing. Or maybe I'm just overly sentimental, knowing full well my delusions have completely abstracted my worldview. It gets harder to listen to music as I feel I'm always changing, always shifting. And maybe I went through a portal that night at the bar, or at least I hope I did. I had been craving change for so long, I was beginning to lose hope, thinking I had to puzzle together how to trigger it myself. Regardless, something did suddenly feel different about home – maybe it was another looming freeze, another Ice Age at the Texican border. And maybe the remaining plants on my porch would die in the cold, or maybe it was all a metaphor. Maybe, maybe, maybe. It could all be hidden within the unsurety of my words.

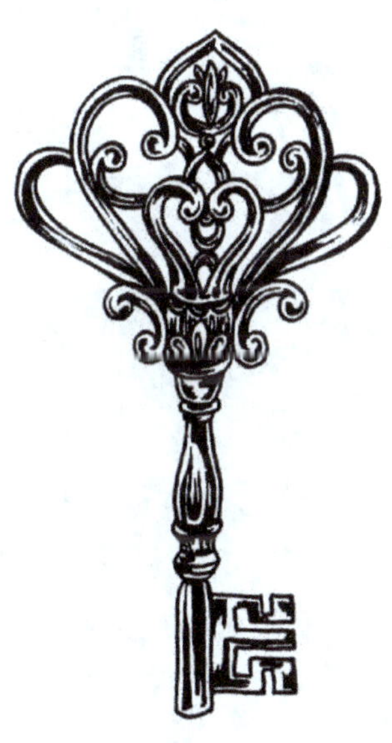

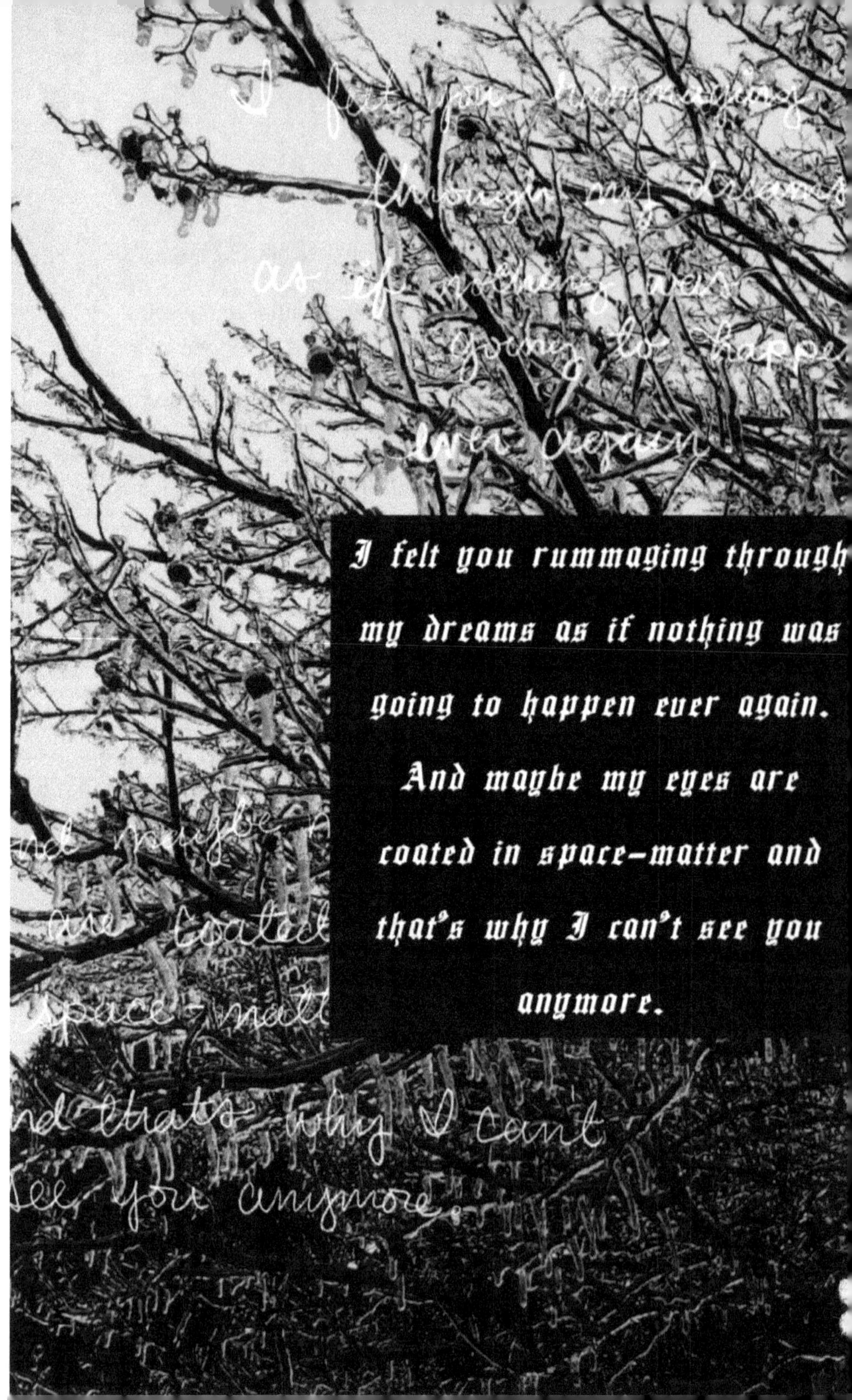
I felt you rummaging through
my dreams as if nothing was
going to happen ever again.
And maybe my eyes are
coated in space-matter and
that's why I can't see you
anymore.

SOME WORDS FROM THE ENVELOPE *

I thought about you with such *fervor* it would make the *celestial* gods cry.
At some point I began to *decompose* from the inside out—
something *sacrilegious* detached and found *egress* through my quivering lips—
asphyxiation.

I would choke so intensely on those *inescapable* feelings, almost *anguish*,
but more an *energetic sadness.*
I found a *rhythmic heart-drumming* at dawn,
having awoken *spellbound* by the images my mind fed me of you—
and at *twilight*, I would lay open and purely exposed,
my creative nerves raw and throbbing—
contemplating my own brutal existence through the delicate fibers of *summer hydrangeas* and *lilies of the valley.*

How I wished to be a flower,
to yearn for the Sun, to be passionately plucked from my roots
to meet the unmarred hands of a child
or the tender embrace of a woman someone loves so deeply—
only to meet my *sanguine demise.*

Instead, I am raw and tender and bloody,
with a body endlessly pulsing,
responsible for the curation of my entire life and met constantly with *aggressiveness.*
Because in my current state,
everyday is a constant nightmarish reminder that I am brutally alive,
brutally human,

and vulnerable to love and loss
solely at the whim of the cosmos and those around me.

My only solace is knowing I was born in the same era as you,
that you are in my world,
and somehow those alchemical thoughts transform me into the flower,
at the mercy of your divine hands.

*reference to the preface

70 CANDLES

Your name stopped
appearing in my phone.
I think maybe it's because
the skies are
just too beautiful over on
your side
of this broken country—
the sunsets are too
distracting and
maybe the stars sing you a
different lullaby
when you gaze
up at the same moon I see.
And when the land is set
ablaze again,
the red skies full of ash,
you focus on covering
your face
on the way to the car
instead of wondering if the
red of that
sky is the same red as my
heart.

I'll wrap myself in the flames
of 70 candles
to feel the warmth I crave
from you.
I'd hate to see who you
follow now
that you've stopped watching
me through
cyberspace – your rare hearts
like
precious gemstones.
And the weight of those 70
candles may
crush me into an
everlasting sleep
where I hope all I dream
about is you.
Because your name stopped
appearing in
my phone and I feel a great
sense of loss.

I'll nod at the spider
that now lives
in my bathroom
because I decided
not to take it out
into the cold,
the same red spider that was
crouched in the corner
of the ceiling
when I came home from
seeing you—
the same red spider
that watched
me scream and bawl
in the bathtub
the following day—
it has watched me all this
December,
day after day.
crying over my 70 candles
as I slowly blow them out
one by one.

If you dream of me,

I'll meet you there;

where the stars form
in the clouds and the
roses softly whisper.

what will you say
to dream me?

maybe I will wake
with your message.

We're all just fabricated from the stars,
a never-ending cosmos -
the universe experiencing itself
through humanity.

And maybe
when I look up at the night sky,
I am looking into a mirror.

And maybe
when I look at my own reflection,
I'm looking into your eyes.

MY FIRST WITHOUT YOU DREAM

The first dream I had of you
without tender love, kissing and caressing,
finally arrived at the threshold
of my mind.

I had an unsettling amount of awareness,
aching and yearning for you
with no speck of reciprocation—
no glimmer of hope.

Something about rotting food and
endless clutter in my childhood bedroom,
and there you sat unmoved and
unentertained in the blue light
of a loft,
with multi-colored Christmas lights
hanging above your head.

And no matter how I tried to look at you,
you never looked back
as if I weren't even there,
a mere apparition watching you
looking pale and expressionless.
I tried all I could to rationalize it
when I finally woke up.

He opened the door to ask if I
made a noise beckoning him,
but I just groaned in my sleep,
maybe out of sadness or frustration.
I felt a deep sense of loss
laying in that bed with
muted morning light.

I must be writing too much about my dreams.
I worried, instantly,
that the Universe was telling me
to let you go—
that there must be no more love
coming to me from the ether.
All I can do is hope that you will return with a heart next time.

THE HILLS

I thought the hills were with you,
But I found them just behind
My field of view,
Blending in with the hazy horizon,
Thinking my eyes were making it
Ridged with the tears that always
Well up when I don't want them to.

I guess you gave the hills to me when I wasn't looking—
Maybe through the soft but swift touch of your hand on mine,
Maybe through the game we played at the bar that night.

The hills lay behind my honey-golden eyes, inside my mouth, peering through my parted lips when I daydream of kissing you.

I hoped, deep down, that those beautiful hills were still with you instead of flooding with the rosé I bought on a whim and sip on every night instead of smoking and eating my weight in gas station snacks.

The rosé helps me write, I suppose – helps me write about those gorgeous hills and the way they glisten when the sun begins to slowly peer up from behind them.

The radiant warmth from these hills remind me of the radiant warmth of your smile, your puffed-up chest, and how eagerly I wanted to graze your lips with my fingertips.

The hills, hills, hills, because the mountains are too far away now, and I haven't seen them in four years. And those hills have been hidden in my teeth for four years, since you handed them to me that night in my dreams, maybe even that night you made me laugh over pizza when my eyes were stretched out and blue with those lines – four years since Winter Solstice by the Bay.

Your hand with those hills; the hand you touched mine with to feel their coldness after my first cigarette in three months – the same hand you use to strum my heartstrings like a true prodigy. Your hands amongst the beautiful hills; your hand that I wish had caressed my face in the pale moonlight.

And those small hills just beyond the shore I saw out of the hotel window.

Oh, how those hills looked so magnificent in your tender eyes – the few times I was able to *actually* look into them. And now they are with me, somehow, drowning in tears and rosé and candle wax I hope you will peel off my skin someday.

The candles inside old wine bottles light up the hills in my yellowing teeth, as the Marlboros pile up in the ashtray outside – cigarette butts with the color of my new lipstick – cherry black or black cherry.

I think the color would look great on your cheek or on your neck if the hills were watching from their little spot in the distance.

I'll claim them as my dominion, but only if you share them with me.

I'd hate to keep planning on how to give them to you when you just hand them right back to me without doing anything significant.

I swam through a dream with you in the city and it was hazy and windy like the hills were this morning.
I wish you could see them now.

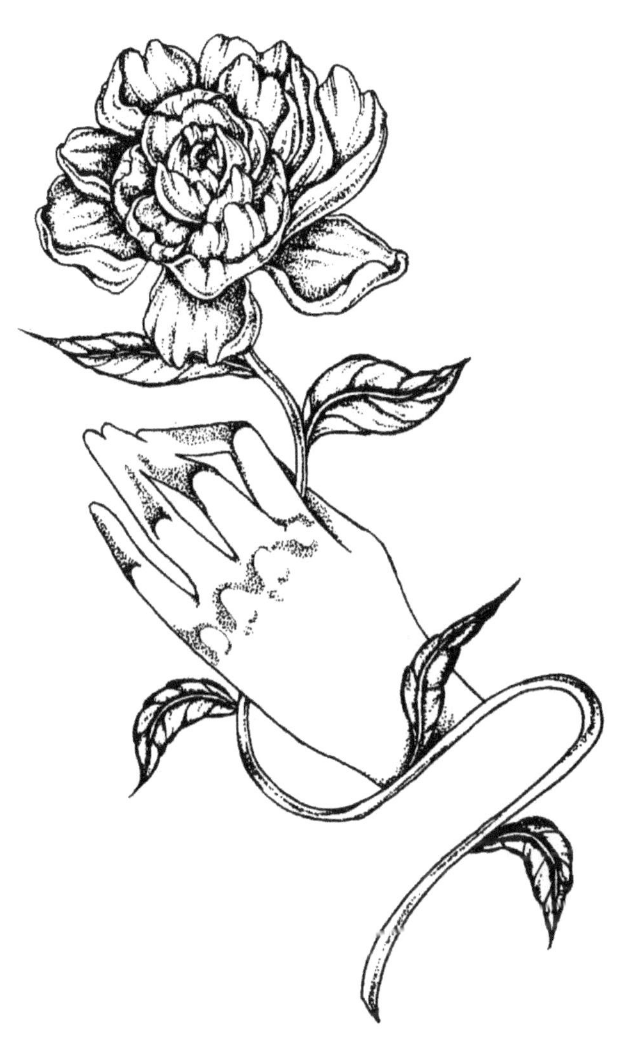

WINTER SOLSTICE

It's almost hard not knowing where we came from,
Not knowing if we have purpose or if nothing really matters.
I'd like to think we were put on this earth together for a reason,
As I don't actually believe in coincidences—
And how the beautiful Bay brought you to me before we even met.

I found a home there, encased in brick and ivy and
The dreams that made me who I am today.
Many times I've changed my mind but you remained consistent—
And I think that's why it was meant to be,
Even if you don't see it.

I dreamed a lucid dream of
Plucking oranges from their trees
And dancing in my yellow skirt on Revere Beach.
If I had cinnamon in my teeth,
Would you kiss me just for the taste?
And if you held me in your arms under the cloudless night sky,
Would the stars watch us dance in their pale silver light?

I dreamed a beautiful dream of
Watching you sing on the stage
With your eyes glimmering at me,
Though I think I felt the coldness in my brittle ribcage
In those lonely neighborhood cigarette walks.

At some point, it was the Solstice again—
The longest night of the year,
And all I wished for under the all-consuming darkness
Was for a new year with you.
Counting the years has become a chore,
Now that I'm getting older.

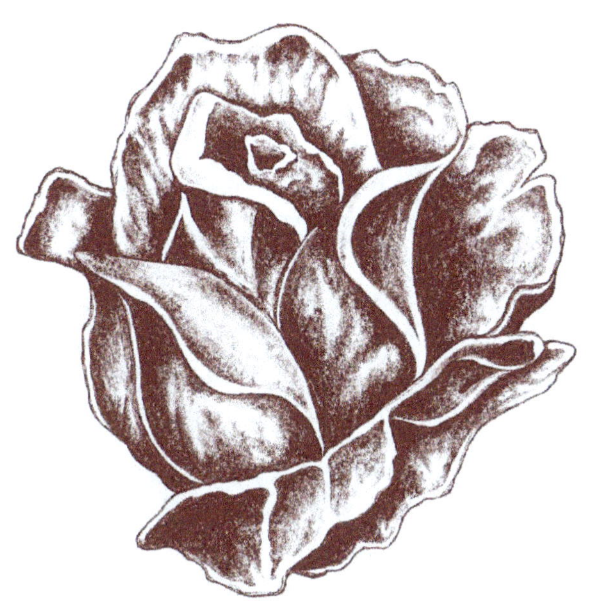

ASHES OF LOVE LETTERS

When I see you now,
I know you are far away—
An ever-growing distance,
And it makes my heart
Sink further and further
Into my stomach,
Like boiling rocks.

And it's that sinking feeling
That makes me believe like I'm
Tied to an anchor and
I'm drowning without
Any sense of control.

I think I will always speculate,
Though I will never truly
Know the reason.

If you were to tell me why
Without it being good,
I might burst—
The water might start
Pouring into my lungs—
Suffocation.

Tonight, I wrote you a
Love letter with
A tender kiss—
And set it ablaze
Under the moonless sky,

Not knowing where
The smoke and ash
Would end up—

Whether the cold air
Would take my burdens away
Into the hands of the
Stars above me or
Carry those whispers
So they may sweetly
Kiss your ears.

And if I drown before they
Reach you,
I hope to feel the loving warmth
Of your hand
At the bottom
Of the Ocean.

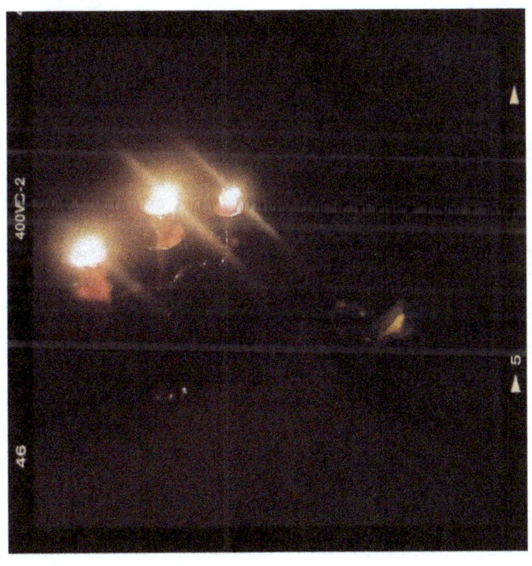

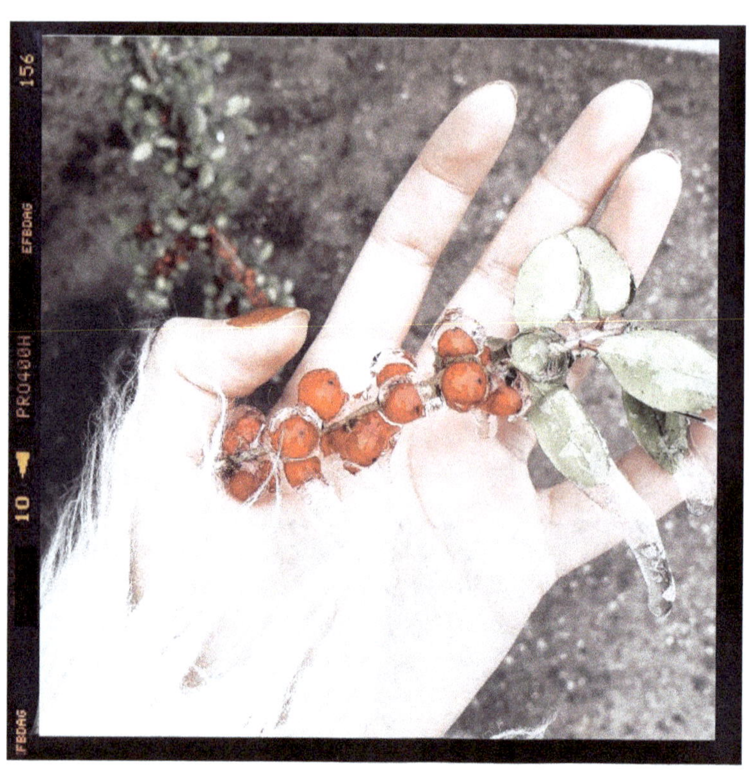
156
EFBDAG
PRO400H
10
FBDAG

PRETTY LIKE THE GIRLS IN CALIFORNIA

I'm not pretty like the girls in California ;;
I know.
I'm not fashionable like the girls in New York ;;
I know.

I used three different appliances in my hair this morning,
And I still want to cry—
the woman who stares back at me
is not pretty like the girls in California,
and I tell her that every day.

I know I'm not desirable like I used to be,
not skinny like I used to be.
My skin is sagging and graying with age,
but I still break out like I'm thirteen.
Expensive skincare products and makeup
have been on my Christmas list every year for several years now,
and nothing changes.

I tell the woman who stares back at me,
"He will never be mesmerized by your beauty
because you have none to offer,"
and I do not cry most of the time—
only when it feels all too real.

I'm not pretty like the girls in California,
or fashionable like the girls in New York,
I know.

Any beauty rituals I perform will all be in vain,
I know.
And Aphrodite hates me for my self-talk ;;

I think I should start praying to her.
Maybe she will grow my lips so they are kissable
and shrink my nose to make it cute.

*If anything, she will teach me to love myself,
because you're not here to do that for me.*

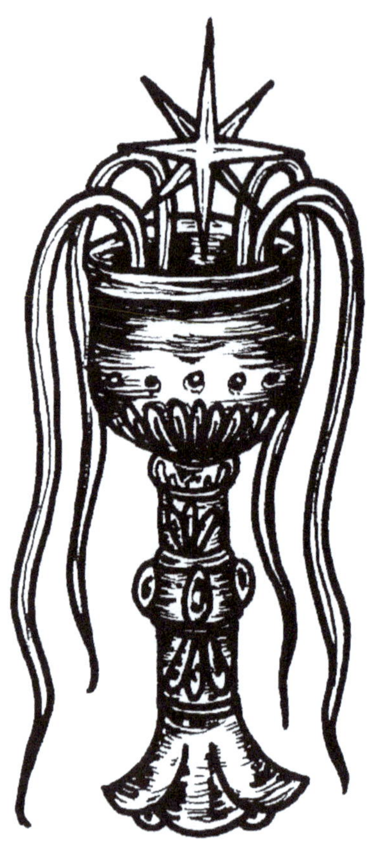

I WAS ONCE A SPRING CHILD

I had been tattered, I suppose,
at least that is how I was found—
under some subtle wreckage with my
skin torn where my limbs met my core ;;
with my honey-glazed eyes glued shut
from the toxins that leaked from
my swollen tear ducts.

That was the last time the Sun came out—
warming my brittle frozen body and
thawing me out from a winter
I never thought would end.

It was quite inviting, welcoming,
though it sadly didn't last long.

If last year was Imbolc in February,
with delicate hints of spring,
this year already feels whole like March.

I am thawing once again
into a world that feels immensely different—
and as more time passes,
the better the air around me feels ;;
feels like love is finally upon me
and my skin is growing stronger
glowing.

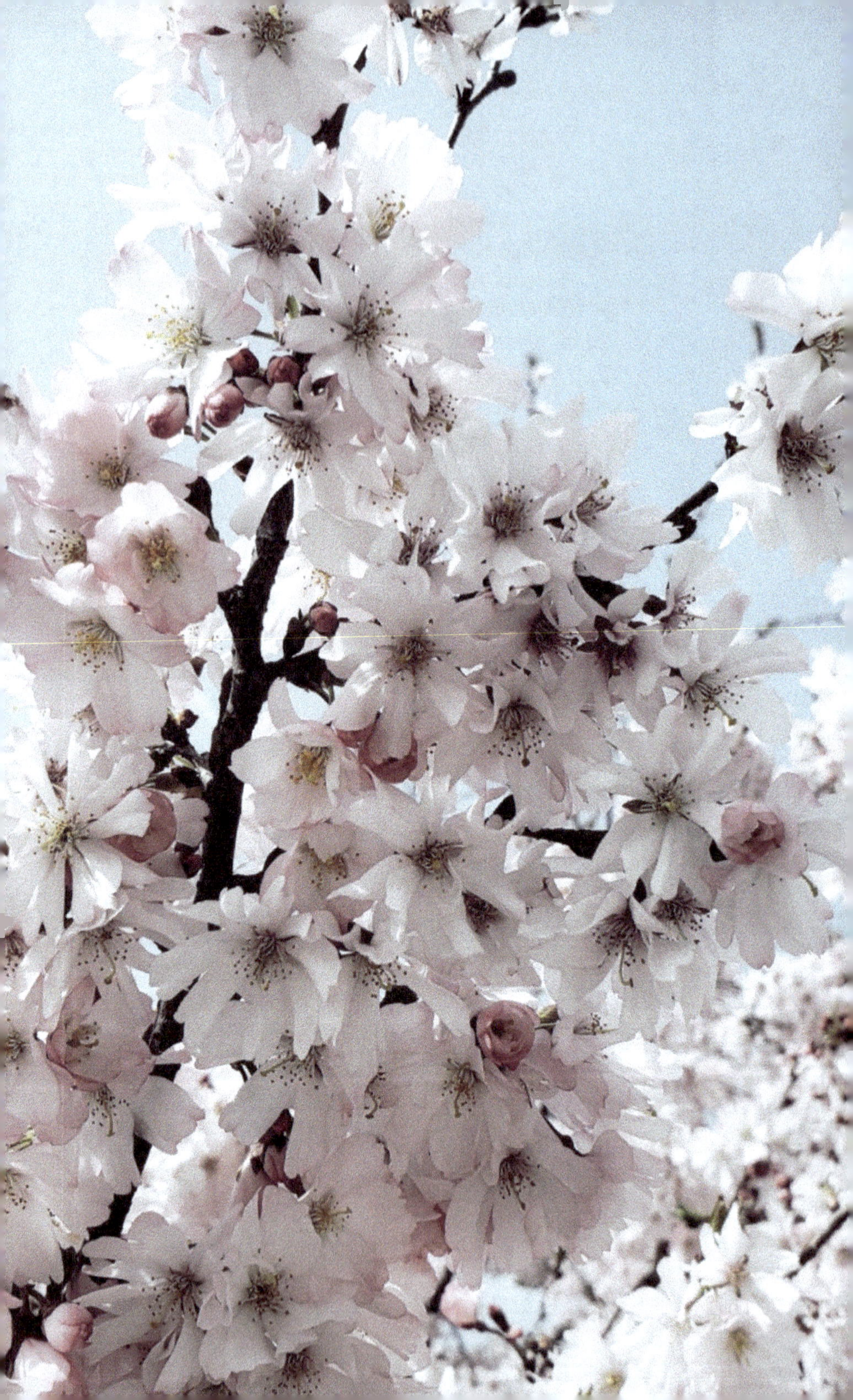

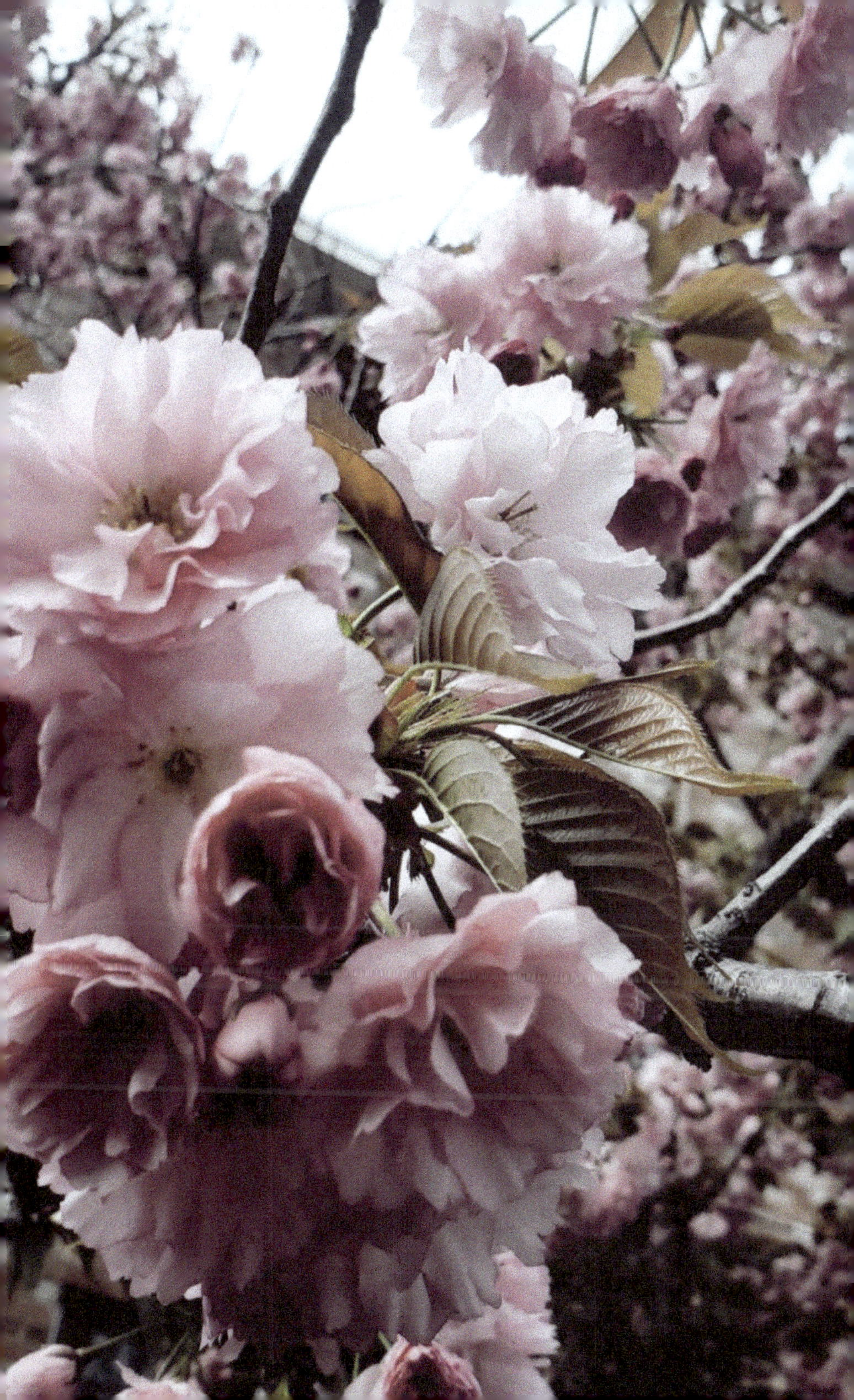

IF IT RAINS AGAIN

After it rains,
The smell emanating from the pavement is sweet
And all I can think about is
Being in your loving embrace.

After it rains,
My tears become indistinguishable from the
Droplets the sky gave us,
And I resent myself for how I feel and
How overcast weather dulls my edges
When I'm meant to be sharp.

You know how sharp I'm supposed to be—
I think we can and should feed each other's flames,
And maybe the rain will subside for good,
Though I don't know how much good that would do,
As the rainwater keeps us tied to Mother Earth
And she is where we met.

Without our tethers,
We might escape the atmosphere—
Floating up towards the stars who might
Kiss us goodnight as the oxygen depletes.

Maybe you're my tether when it rains,
Though I'm not sure what the landscape
Of your mind is really like.

I know it will rain again,
And when it does,
I hope you're there to be my shelter,
The place I can call home—
With my ear against your beating heart,
And maybe I'll never shed another tear
Ever again.

the magnolias are different here

and maybe I am too

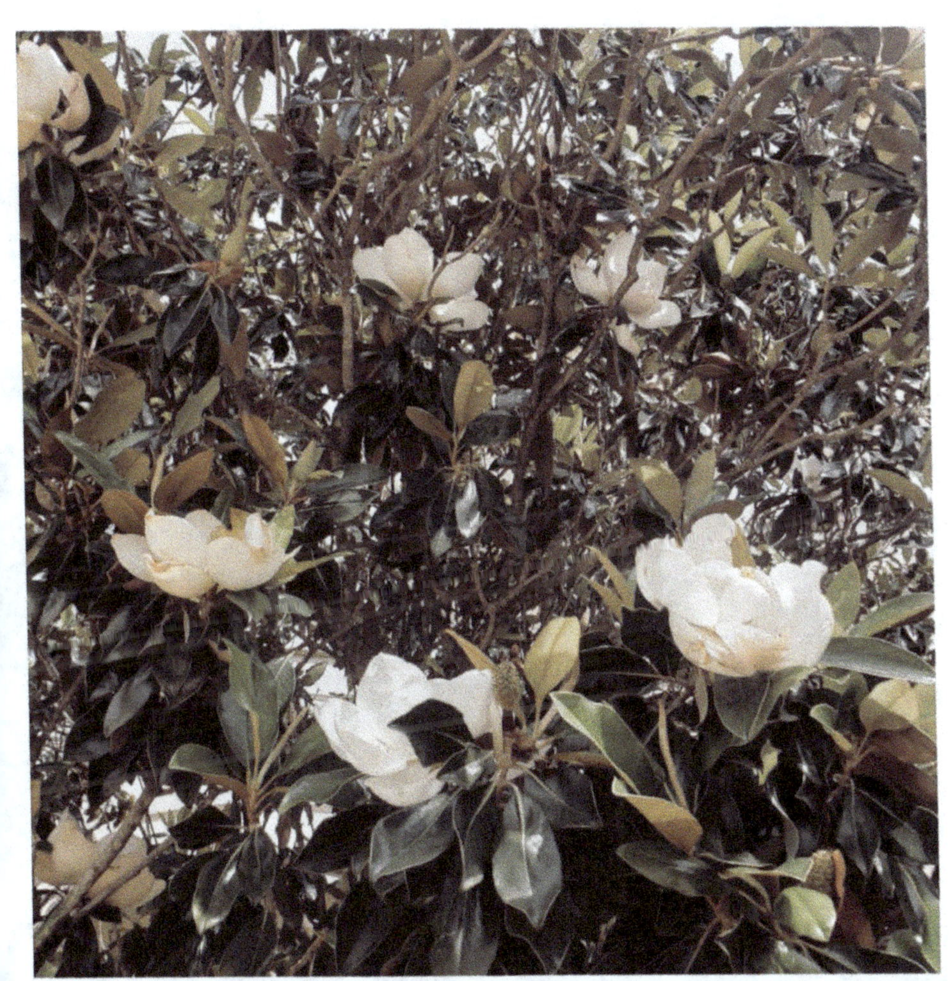

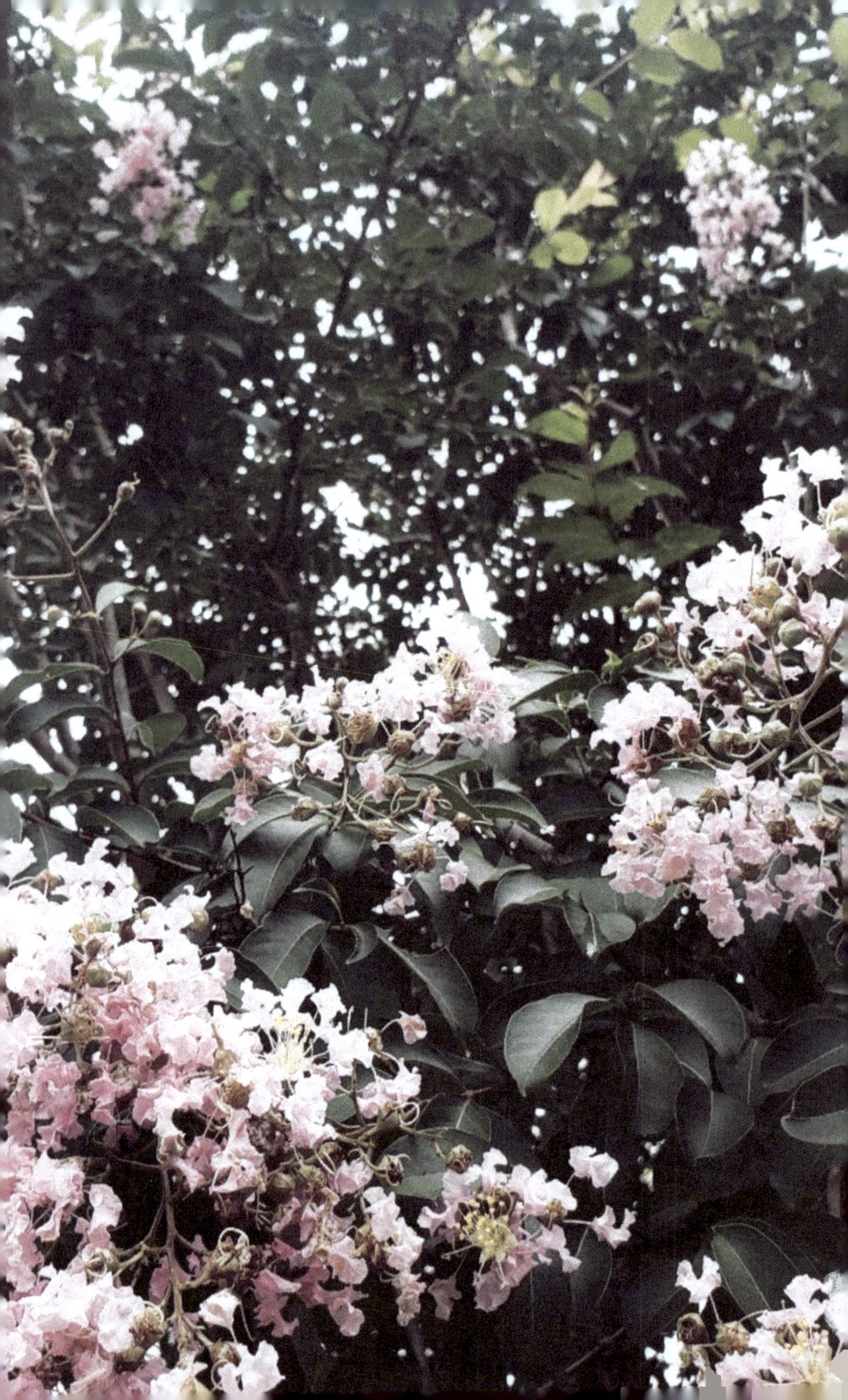

EPILOGUE - I AM NEWNESS

It's starting to feel like spring again
in the way that
there's a sense of newness in the air
and rebirth is on the horizon.

Death came knocking at my chamber door
with his hood covering his delicate face
and sliced through the chess pieces
carefully laid out on my bed with his scythe.
I never thought the night would end,
but his gesture reminded me that
nothing lasts forever—
not even You and Me.

Life rose with the Sun,
illuminating all my dusty winter branches
and showed me where to sprout my blossoms from.

Ethereal. Unreal.

You are miles away in many different ways,
and it aches within my birdcage frame
to feel your distance.

I will grow my glowing blossoms towards the Sun
and stretch my branches out so they may bear fruit for the Moon.
I will not shatter my limbs
or pull at my starving roots—
I will allow myself to grow with this new Vernal Season,
and if you notice my newfound beauty,
then so be it.

But I will be here,
twisting myself towards the cosmos
regardless.

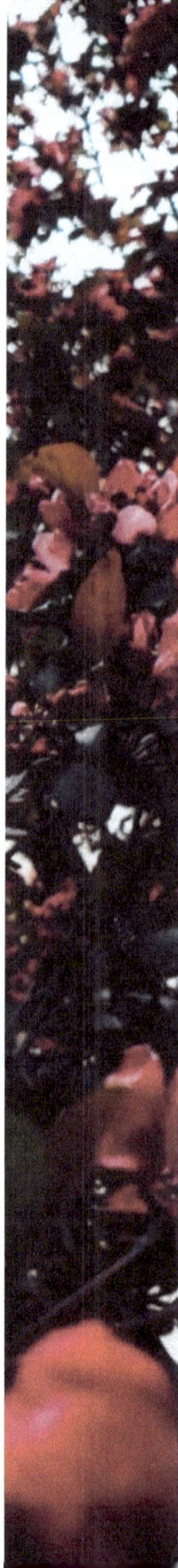

you are so beautiful now,

you shine brighter than

The Star

and now I am blind.

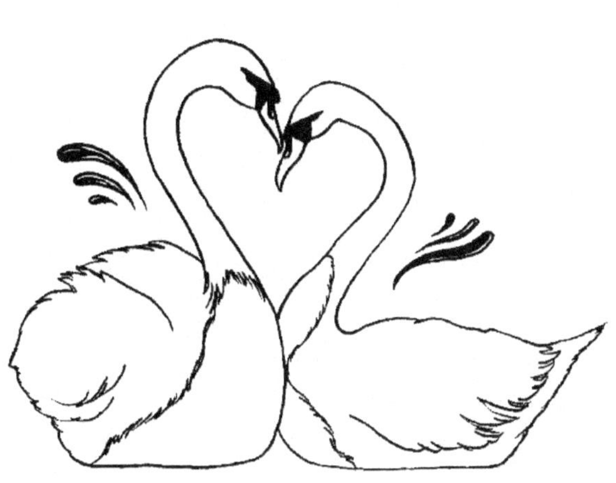

NOTES

PHOTOS (in order of appearance)
Magnolia Tree; Boston, MA; 2019
Wall Details of Boston Public Library; Boston, MA, 2022
Blossom Tree; Boston, MA; 2019
Neighborhood FBC Church; Pflugerville, TX; 2023
Red Berry Tree; Austin, TX; 2023
Church of the Covenant; Boston, MA; 2022
Carnations in Candlelight; Austin, TX, 2023
Satanic Graffiti on a Building; Salt Lake City, UT; 2013
The Witch House; Salem, MA; 2019
Rose Bush; Austin, TX; 2023
Chrysanthemum at Isabella Stewart Gardner Museum; Boston, MA; 2019
White Wildflowers; Clifton, VA; 2020
Red Berry Tree during Winter Freeze; Austin, TX; 2023
Prudential Building during Sunset; Boston, MA; 2019
Grey Shore; Nahant, MA; 2020
Roses at the Gas Station; Austin, TX; 2023
White Azaleas; Clifton, VA; 2020
Red Berry Bush; Clifton, VA; 2020
Magnolia Tree; Boston, MA; 2019
Rose Bush; Austin, TX; 2023
Stained Glass at Isabella Stewart Gardner Museum; Boston, MA; 2019
Stain Glass at Boston Museum of Fine Arts; Boston, MA; 2019
Cityscape; Boston, MA; 2019
Back Bay from The Fens; Boston, MA; 2019
Power Lines; Austin, TX, 2023
Texas Sky; Round Rock, TX; 2021
Branches in Winter Freeze; Austin, TX, 2023
Sunset Clouds; Round Rock, TX; 2021
Full Moon; Austin, TX; 2022
Distorted Prudential; Boston, MA; 2018
Blossom Tree; Boston, MA; 2019
Blossom Tree; Boston, MA, 2019

REFERENCES (in order)

To The End of The Earth - Title Page; Reference to “End of the Earth” by Marina Diamandis

Feral Love - Title Page; Reference to “Feral Love” by Chelsea Wolfe

Stargirl- Title Page; Reference to “Stargirl Interlude” by The Weeknd feat. Lana Del Rey

St James Infirmary Blues; Reference to “St James Infirmary” by Cab Calloway

The Love Witch; Poem & Artwork; Reference to “The Love Witch” dir. Anna Biller

Turn Me Into A Flower - Title Page; Reference to “God Turn Me Into a Flower” by Weyes Blood

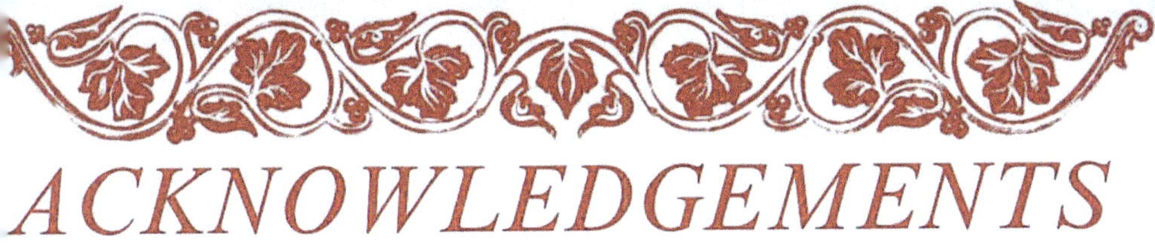

ACKNOWLEDGEMENTS

The biggest and warmest of thank-yous to Kayleigh and Gabe for being my loving and supportive beta readers and helping me edit something so personal. It's one thing to gush onto empty pages and it's a whole other thing to sift through someone else's raw and borderline-disturbing material.

The biggest and warmest of thank-yous to my sweet parents for being so supportive of me and my numerous creative endeavors. When I told them "I'm writing a book," they didn't sigh or roll their eyes, just poured an unending amount of love and support into me and my ideas and I will always be eternally grateful for them.

Thank you to my lovely girl-friends who always listen me talk about the things that haunt my dreams; my lovely girl-friends who read my absurd texts; my lovely girl-friends who read the stars with me and fill me to the brim with magic.

(An extra-special thank you to Kayleigh for allowing me to lay pathetically on her couch, holding her crystals to my aching heart, while I was a raw nerve at the start of the birthing process for this.)

And of course, thank you, my readers, for caressing these pages and consuming their content. I hope you enjoyed this heavy piece of my inner world.

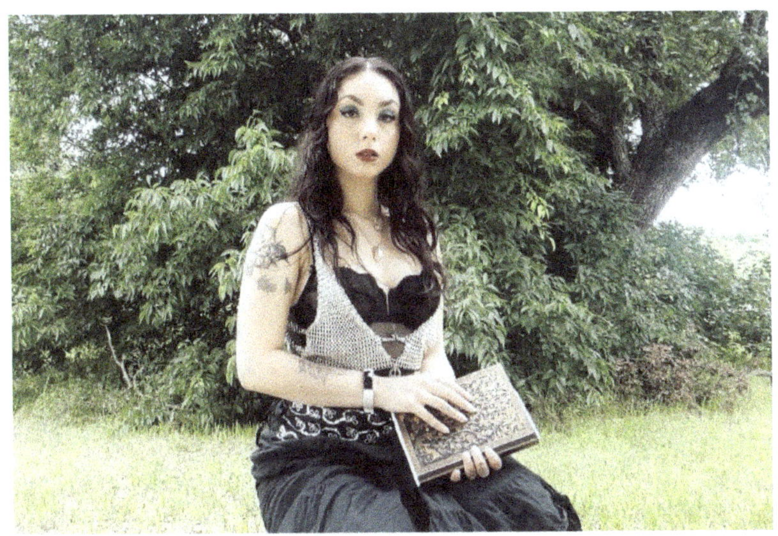

Zoë Riches is a visual artist and poet based in the United States. Her work typically reflects her deepest desires and general outlook on life, often focusing on yearning, heartache, romance, vulnerability, hedonism, and divine femininity.

www.zoerichesart.com
@zoeriches_

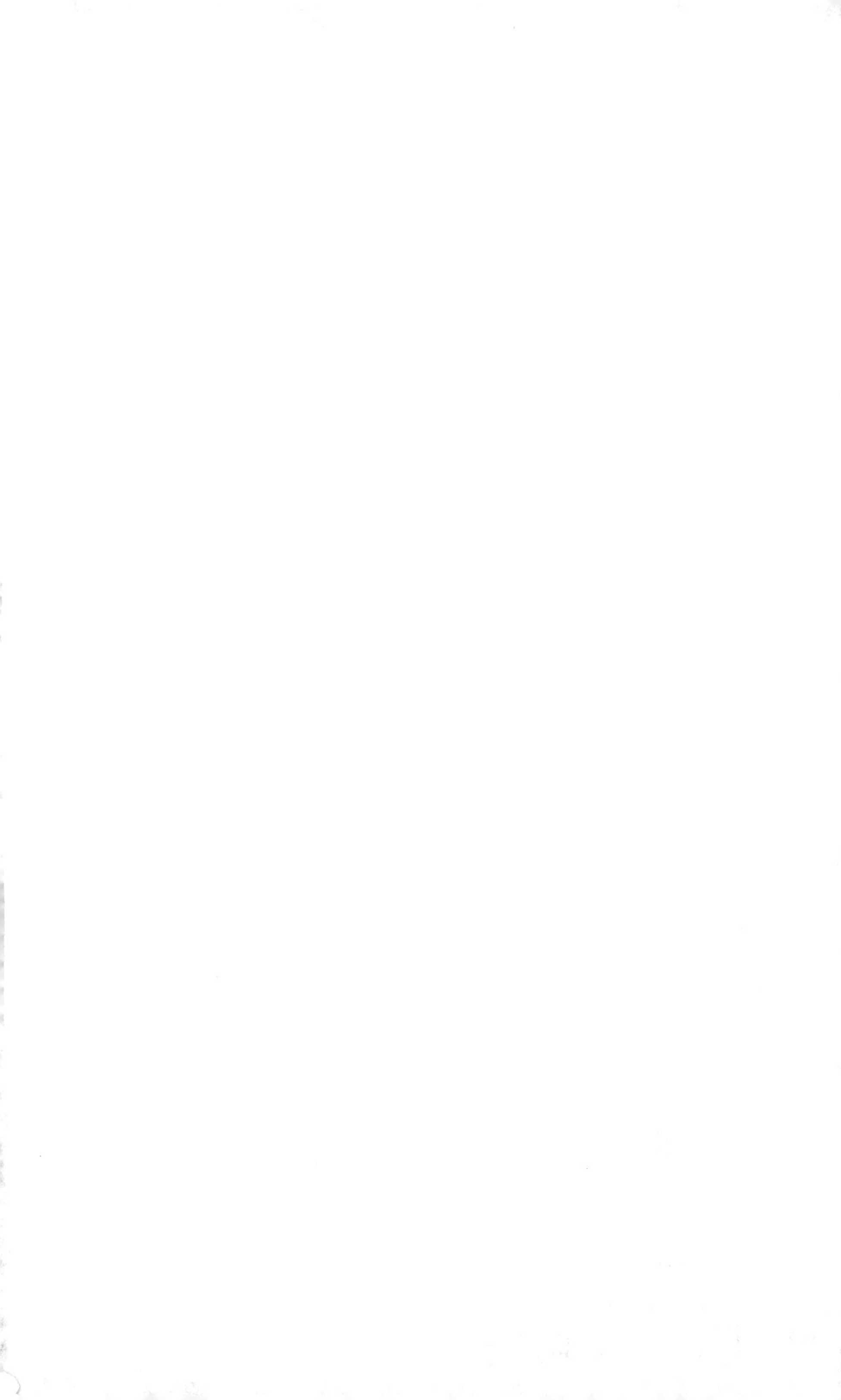

www.ingramcontent.com/pod-product-compliance
Lightning Source LLC
LaVergne TN
LVHW020510100826
845148LV00003B/744

* 9 7 9 8 2 1 8 3 1 6 7 7 8 *